Artificial Narrow Intelligence (ANI)

Understanding the AI Systems That Power Today's World

By Susie Hala

AI Educator | Author | Founder of the IntelliGloss Education Series

IntelliGloss Press

United States of America

Legal Disclaimer

Educational Purpose Disclaimer

"This publication is part of the IntelliGloss AI Education Series, a structured curriculum support system for AI literacy in grades 6–12."

The information presented in this publication is provided for educational and informational purposes only. This book is intended to support educators, administrators, parents, and learners in understanding the concepts, opportunities, and challenges associated with artificial intelligence in education. It is not intended to serve as legal, technical, policy, cybersecurity, or professional advice.

Readers should consult qualified professionals, institutional guidelines, and local regulations before implementing any educational programs, technologies, or policies described in this book.

Technology and Accuracy Disclaimer
Artificial intelligence is a rapidly evolving field. While every effort has been made to ensure the accuracy and reliability of the information presented at the time of publication, technologies, policies, research findings, and best practices may change over time. The author and publisher make no guarantees that all information will remain current or applicable in future technological environments.

Readers are encouraged to verify tools, platforms, and recommendations independently before using them in educational settings.

Implementation Responsibility
Schools, educators, and institutions are solely responsible for determining how and whether to implement artificial intelligence tools, strategies, or classroom activities discussed in this book. Educational environments vary widely, and policies regarding technology use, student privacy, and curriculum development differ by district, state, and country.

The author and publisher assume no responsibility for outcomes resulting from the implementation of ideas, examples, or frameworks described in this book.

Student Safety and Data Privacy
Artificial intelligence tools may involve the collection or processing of data. Educators and institutions are responsible for ensuring that any technology used complies with applicable student privacy laws, data protection regulations, and school policies, including but not limited to FERPA, COPPA, GDPR, or other relevant regulations depending on jurisdiction.

The author and publisher are not responsible for the privacy practices, security policies, or data handling procedures of third-party platforms or software mentioned in this book.

Third-Party Tools and References
This book may reference third-party technologies, organizations, research studies, or platforms for illustrative and educational purposes. Such references do not constitute endorsements or guarantees regarding the performance, reliability, safety, or suitability of those tools for educational use.

Educators and institutions should conduct their own evaluations and risk assessments before adopting any technology.

No Professional Liability
The author and publisher shall not be held liable for any direct, indirect, incidental, or consequential damages resulting from the use or misuse of the information contained in this book. This includes but is not limited to decisions related to curriculum design, technology adoption, classroom instruction, institutional policies, or educational outcomes.

Educational Interpretation
The concepts and examples provided in this book are intended to support discussion and learning. They should not be interpreted as official standards, mandatory guidelines, or universally applicable policies for artificial intelligence education.

Schools and educators are encouraged to adapt the ideas presented here according to their local policies, cultural context, educational standards, and student needs.

Author's Intent
The goal of this book is to promote responsible AI literacy, thoughtful discussion, and ethical awareness as schools prepare students for a world increasingly shaped by intelligent technologies.

The author encourages readers to approach artificial intelligence education with curiosity, caution, and a commitment to responsible learning.

Title: Artificial Narrow Intelligence (ANI) :*Understanding the AI Systems That Power Today's World*

ISBN: 978-1-972925-04-1

Published by
IntelliGloss Press
United States of America

Dedication

This book is dedicated to the next generation of learners—
the students who will grow up in a world shaped by intelligent technology,
and who deserve to understand it with clarity, confidence, and purpose.

To the educators who show up every day with dedication and heart,
guiding students through a rapidly changing world—
your role has never been more important.

To the parents and families who support learning at home,
encouraging curiosity, responsibility, and growth—
you are the foundation of every child's success.

And to my granddaughters,
whose curiosity, imagination, and future inspire me to do this work—
this book is for you.

May you not only learn how to use technology,
but understand it, question it, and shape it for the good of others.

About the Author

Susie Hala
Founder of the IntelliGloss AI Education Series

Susie Hala is an author, educator, and curriculum developer dedicated to advancing artificial intelligence literacy in education. Her work focuses on helping schools, educators, and students understand how intelligent technologies are shaping modern society—and why that understanding is essential for the next generation.

Hala is the creator of the IntelliGloss AI Education Series, a comprehensive and growing collection of educational books designed to make complex artificial intelligence concepts accessible, structured, and practical for classroom use. Her work emphasizes clarity, organization, and responsible implementation, enabling schools to introduce AI literacy without requiring advanced technical backgrounds.

In addition to her work in education, Hala brings hands-on experience working with artificial intelligence systems, including early exposure to rule-based AI technologies during her time working with AT&T. She has also developed modern digital platforms that integrate artificial intelligence, automation, and online systems, building e-commerce solutions and AI-driven applications that connect payment platforms, hosting environments, and conversational AI tools into real-world, functional systems.

This combination of foundational understanding and practical experience allows her to translate complex AI concepts into clear, accessible language for both educators and students.

Recognizing that artificial intelligence is rapidly transforming how information is created, interpreted, and used, Hala advocates for equipping students with the ability not only to use AI tools, but to understand, question, and evaluate them. Her work emphasizes critical thinking, ethical awareness, and responsible digital citizenship.

The IntelliGloss AI Education Series supports schools in teaching key areas such as artificial intelligence foundations, algorithms, machine learning concepts, and AI ethics, as well as the broader evolution of intelligent systems—from Artificial Narrow Intelligence (ANI) to Artificial General Intelligence (AGI) and Artificial Superintelligence (ASI). These resources are designed for students in grades 6–12 and for educators seeking structured, classroom-ready approaches to AI literacy.

In addition to her work in education publishing, Hala has a strong background in entrepreneurship, having built and managed multiple businesses and educational initiatives. Her experience across industries reinforces her belief that technology education must remain grounded in human values, critical thinking, and ethical responsibility.

Her mission is clear: to ensure that the next generation understands intelligent technology—not just how to use it, but how it truly works.

Preface

Two Students. Two Paths. One Future.

Before we begin, it is important to understand why learning how artificial intelligence works—not just how to use it—matters for every student.

Imagine two students who have just graduated from high school and are preparing for a job interview. The first student knows how to use artificial intelligence tools. This student can generate answers, complete assignments quickly, and rely on AI to assist with tasks. However, this student does not understand how artificial intelligence works behind the scenes.

The second student also knows how to use AI tools, but in addition, understands the foundational concepts behind them. This student has learned about data, algorithms, tokens, models, and how intelligent systems are trained and operate. This student can think critically about AI, recognize its limitations, and adapt when needed.

At first, the first student may appear faster and more efficient. However, over time, the second student demonstrates a deeper level of understanding, independence, and problem-solving ability. The second student is not only able to use artificial intelligence but also to question it, improve it, and grow with it.

This book is written for the second student.

In a world where artificial intelligence is becoming part of everyday life, students must not only learn how to use intelligent systems—they must learn how they work. True understanding leads to confidence, responsibility, and the ability to lead in an AI-driven future.

This perspective is not just theoretical—it is personal.

There was a time when I was the first student.

I knew how to use systems. I followed processes, completed tasks, and worked within structured environments that required accuracy and consistency. At the time, I did not think of these systems as artificial intelligence. They were simply part of the job—tools that had to be learned, followed, and mastered.

But looking back, I now understand something much deeper. I was working within rule-based systems—the earliest foundation of what we now recognize as artificial intelligence.

That realization changed everything.

As I began studying modern AI, including machine learning, deep learning, and intelligent systems, I started to see a clear connection between the past and the present. The structured systems I once worked in, the logic behind decision-making, and the step-by-step processes all still exist today. They have simply evolved.

Artificial intelligence did not appear overnight. It grew from rule-based systems into systems that can now learn, adapt, and assist in ways we never imagined.

I made a decision to move from simply using systems to understanding them.

That journey—from student one to student two—is the reason these books exist.

My mission is to help others bridge that same gap.

I believe that artificial intelligence should be understandable for everyone. It should not feel intimidating or out of reach. Students should feel confident exploring it. Teachers should feel prepared to introduce it. Everyday learners should have access to clear, structured explanations that make sense.

You do not need a background in technology. You do not need to know how to code. You only need the right explanation.

A Note from the Author

AI Is a Tool — Not a Decision Maker

Artificial Intelligence is becoming part of everyday life. Students use it to complete assignments, teachers use it to support instruction, and businesses use it to improve efficiency. While these tools are powerful and useful, there is an important truth that must remain clear from the very beginning:

Artificial Intelligence does not make decisions—people do.

One of the main purposes of this book is to help readers understand how AI works, what it can do, and—just as importantly—what it cannot do. AI systems are designed to process information, identify patterns, and generate responses based on data. They can assist with thinking, but they do not think independently. They can provide answers, but they do not understand consequences. They can suggest ideas, but they do not choose actions.

Every outcome that involves AI begins and ends with human involvement. A person asks the question. A person reviews the response. A person decides what to do next. Responsibility does not transfer to the machine.

In today's world, it is easy to confuse speed with intelligence and automation with authority. Because AI can respond quickly and confidently, it may appear as though it is making decisions. In reality, it is performing a task based on patterns it has learned—not exercising judgment.

This distinction matters. When people begin to rely on AI without understanding its role, they risk misunderstanding information, misusing technology, or placing trust in a system that is not capable of accountability. Clear understanding leads to responsible use.

This book was written to remove confusion and provide clarity. It is designed to help students and educators move beyond simply using AI tools and begin understanding the structure behind them. By learning how AI supports human thinking—rather than replacing it—readers can approach technology with confidence, awareness, and responsibility.

Artificial Intelligence is a powerful assistant. It can enhance learning, support creativity, and improve productivity. But it remains a tool.

The decisions, the actions, and the responsibility will always belong to the human.

— Susie Hala

The Purpose of This Book

This book is built on a simple but essential principle:

Students should not only use artificial intelligence—they should understand it.

By clearly defining core concepts such as chatbots, generative AI, agentic AI, autonomy, and the continuum of AI use, this curriculum provides a structured pathway for developing both technical understanding and critical thinking.

Artificial intelligence is not a single tool or system. It is a collection of capabilities that must be understood in context.

Clarity is the foundation of responsible innovation.

The IntelliGloss Instructional Approach

The IntelliGloss AI Education Series is designed to help students move beyond simply using AI tools and begin understanding artificial intelligence as a complete system.

Students learn how AI is built, how it operates, and how it connects to the real world.

Why Artificial Intelligence Education Matters for Every Student

Why AI Literacy Is Essential for Every Student

Artificial intelligence is no longer a future concept or a specialized technology used only by experts. It is already part of everyday life for students of all ages. From smartphones and search engines to navigation apps, social media, streaming platforms, and educational tools, AI systems influence how information is accessed, decisions are made, and learning takes place.

Because AI is embedded in daily life, understanding it is no longer optional. It is a foundational skill, similar to digital literacy and critical thinking. Students do not need to become programmers or engineers, but they do need to understand what AI is, how it works at a basic level, and how it affects their lives.

AI education should not be limited to computer science classrooms. Every student interacts with AI systems daily. Teaching students how these systems function empowers them to become informed users rather than passive consumers of technology.

This book is designed to make artificial intelligence understandable, approachable, and relevant. It focuses on clarity, responsibility, and real-world understanding to help students prepare for a future where humans and intelligent systems work side by side.

IntelliGloss AI Education Series

Teaching how AI actually works—from hardware to power to global systems.

Why AI Education Matters

Artificial intelligence is already shaping how students learn, write, research, and solve problems.

Yet many students—and educators—are using AI tools without understanding how these systems actually work.

Schools need more than access to technology.
They need structured, responsible AI education.

Our Approach

The IntelliGloss AI Education Series is designed to help students move beyond simply using AI tools and begin understanding artificial intelligence as a complete system.

Students learn how AI is built, how it operates, and how it connects to the real world.

The IntelliGloss Framework

Our books introduce AI through a clear and connected system:

Chip Family — the hardware that powers AI

Watts Family — the rate at which AI uses power

Energy Family — the total power AI consumes over time

Infrastructure Family — the global systems that support AI

This framework helps students understand AI from the inside out.

Built for the Classroom

Each book includes:

Structured chapters aligned with semester learning

Clear explanations designed for student understanding

Reflection sections with learning objectives

Worksheets, quizzes, and answer keys

Teacher Implementation Guides

Supporting Schools and Educators

The IntelliGloss series supports:

Responsible and ethical AI use

Student data awareness and safety

Critical thinking and digital literacy

Classroom-ready instruction for grades 6–12 and beyond

What This Book Is—and What It Is Not

Many people today are becoming familiar with artificial intelligence through tools like ChatGPT, Microsoft Copilot, Canva, and other AI-powered applications. These tools can help with writing, answering questions, creating images, and completing everyday tasks.

In addition to these tools, you may also hear terms such as **AI agents, agentic AI, autonomous systems, and generative AI**. While these may sound complex, they are all part of the same evolving landscape of artificial intelligence technologies.

This book is not a guide on how to use those tools.

Instead, it explains what makes those tools possible.

Behind every AI tool is a system made up of multiple layers working together. At the most basic level, information is represented as bits and processed through powerful computer chips. That information is organized into data, broken into tokens, and then processed by algorithms and models that allow the system to recognize patterns, generate responses, and perform tasks.

These components—chips, bits, tokens, data, algorithms, and models—work together as a complete system. While users may only see the tool, the real intelligence comes from how these underlying parts interact behind the scenes.

Artificial intelligence can also be understood in terms of different levels of capability. Most of the AI systems used today fall under **Artificial Narrow Intelligence (ANI)**, which is designed to perform specific tasks, such as answering questions or generating content. More advanced forms, such as **Artificial General Intelligence (AGI)** and **Artificial Superintelligence (ASI)** represent future possibilities where AI could match or exceed human-level thinking. While these advanced levels are still theoretical, understanding the differences helps provide a broader view of where AI is today and where it may be heading.

For students, parents, and educators, this distinction is important. Learning how to use AI tools is helpful, but understanding how they work—and where they fit within the larger AI landscape—builds stronger thinking, better decision-making, and more responsible use.

Most importantly, artificial intelligence does not make decisions on its own. It does not take responsibility for actions or outcomes. AI systems generate responses based on data and patterns, but it is always the human who decides what to do with that information.

This book is designed to make these underlying systems clear and accessible, even for readers who are new to artificial intelligence.

Artificial intelligence is still in its early stages of development. As these technologies continue to grow, those who understand the foundation behind them will be better prepared to adapt, question, and use them wisely.

Who This Book Is For

This book is designed for educators, school leaders, and curriculum developers guiding students in an age of rapidly advancing technology.

Artificial intelligence is already influencing how students learn, research, and communicate. Yet many educators have not received formal training in how these systems work or how they should be addressed in the classroom.

This book helps bridge that gap by providing clear explanations and practical frameworks for understanding artificial intelligence in an educational setting.

How Schools Can Use This Book

This book supports schools in developing a structured approach to artificial intelligence literacy.

It can be used for:

- Professional development for educators
- Classroom discussions and activities
- Curriculum support across subject areas
- Policy and academic integrity conversations

Rather than focusing on specific tools, this book emphasizes lasting principles that help students understand, evaluate, and use AI responsibly.

Closing Perspective

Artificial intelligence will continue to evolve. With the right knowledge and leadership, schools can ensure that students not only use these technologies, but understand them, question them, and apply them responsibly.

IntelliGloss is more than a book series. It is a structured approach to preparing students for a future shaped by artificial intelligence.

Rather than focusing only on how to use AI tools, this series helps students understand how AI actually works—from its foundational building blocks to real-world applications.

"Before exploring the technical structure of artificial intelligence, it is equally important to understand the human principles that guide its use."

How to Use This Book Responsibly

This book is designed to help students, educators, and readers better understand the growing world of artificial intelligence and modern technology. The purpose of this book is to encourage learning, curiosity, critical thinking, creativity, and responsible technology use in today's digital world.

As artificial intelligence becomes more common in education and everyday life, it is important to understand that AI systems are tools designed to assist humans with learning, research, communication, creativity, and problem-solving. Like all technologies, AI systems should be used thoughtfully and responsibly.

Readers are encouraged to:

ask questions,

think critically,

verify important information,

respect diverse perspectives,

use technology responsibly,

and apply good judgment when working with digital tools and AI systems.

This book supports responsible learning and encourages readers to become informed, thoughtful, and ethical participants in an AI-driven world. The goal is not only to learn about technology, but also to understand how to use it wisely, safely, and responsibly.

— *IntelliGloss AI Education Series*

Human Values Family

Definition

The Human Values Family in artificial intelligence represents the guiding principles that shape how AI systems are created, used, and integrated into society. These values include ethics, responsibility, trust, and human well-being.

Artificial intelligence may be built on data, algorithms, and computational systems, but its true impact is measured by how it affects people. For this reason, AI is not only a technical system—it is a human-centered system.

Key Concepts

The Human Values Family exists to ensure that artificial intelligence serves humanity in a positive and responsible way. While AI systems can process information and generate outcomes, they do not possess judgment, empathy, or moral understanding.

This means that human values must guide every stage of AI development—from design to deployment.

AI reflects the intentions, decisions, and assumptions of the people who build and use it. If those values are not carefully considered, AI systems can unintentionally produce biased, harmful, or misleading results.

Understanding human values in AI is not optional—it is essential.

Core Elements of the Human Values Family

Ethics
Ethics in AI refers to making decisions that are fair, just, and respectful of human rights. This includes minimizing bias, protecting privacy, and ensuring transparency in how systems operate.

Responsibility
Responsibility means that humans remain accountable for AI systems. Developers, educators, organizations, and users must take ownership of how AI is used and the outcomes it produces.

Trust
Trust is critical for the successful adoption of AI. People must feel confident that AI systems are reliable, safe, and aligned with their best interests.

Human Well-Being
AI should enhance human life—not replace, harm, or diminish it. This includes supporting learning, improving access to information, and creating opportunities while maintaining human dignity.

Real-World Connection

Artificial intelligence is already influencing how people learn, communicate, and make decisions. From search engines to classroom tools, AI is shaping daily experiences.

Without clear human values guiding these systems, there is a risk of reinforcing misinformation, bias, or unrealistic expectations.

For students, this means learning not only how to use AI tools, but how to question them, evaluate their outputs, and understand their limitations.

Applications in Education

In the classroom, the Human Values Family helps students develop critical thinking and ethical awareness. Teachers can use this framework to guide discussions about fairness, responsibility, and the impact of technology on society.

Students can explore questions such as:

How should AI be used responsibly?

What makes an AI system fair?

How does technology influence human behavior?

This approach supports both technical understanding and responsible decision-making.

Benefits

Teaching human values in AI helps students:

- Develop ethical awareness
- Strengthen critical thinking
- Understand the societal impact of technology
- Become responsible users and future creators of AI

It ensures that learning about AI goes beyond functionality and includes responsibility.

Challenges

Human values are not always universal. Different cultures, communities, and individuals may have different perspectives on what is considered fair or ethical.

Additionally, AI technology is evolving rapidly, often faster than policies and guidelines can keep up. This makes it essential for educators and students to stay informed and adaptable.

Summary

The Human Values Family reminds us that artificial intelligence is not just about machines—it is about people.

By focusing on ethics, responsibility, trust, and human well-being, students can learn to use AI thoughtfully and responsibly.

Understanding these principles helps prepare learners to navigate a world where artificial intelligence plays an increasingly important role in everyday life.

Executive Summary

IntelliGloss AI Education Series

Teaching How Artificial Intelligence Actually Works

Artificial intelligence is already shaping how students learn, write, research, and make decisions. Yet in many classrooms, students are being introduced to AI tools without understanding how these systems actually function.

This creates a critical gap.

Students may become efficient users of technology, but without foundational knowledge, they are not equipped to think critically, evaluate outputs, or use AI responsibly. As AI continues to expand across every industry, this gap will only grow more significant.

The **IntelliGloss AI Education Series** was created to address this challenge.

The Problem

Most current approaches to AI in education focus on tool usage rather than system understanding. As a result:

- Students rely on AI without understanding its limitations
- Educators lack structured frameworks for teaching AI concepts
- Key terms such as generative AI, agentic AI, and autonomy are often introduced without clear definitions
- Responsibility and ethical use are not consistently emphasized

Without clarity, artificial intelligence becomes difficult to teach, difficult to learn, and difficult to manage in a school environment.

The Solution

The IntelliGloss AI Education Series provides a structured, classroom-ready approach to artificial intelligence literacy for grades 6–12.

Rather than focusing on individual tools, this series teaches students how AI works as a complete system—from foundational components to real-world applications.

Students learn to move beyond surface-level interaction and develop true understanding.

The IntelliGloss Framework

The series introduces AI through a clear and connected structure, including:

- Foundational building blocks such as data, algorithms, tokens, and models
- System-level understanding through categories such as intelligence level, behavior, and control
- Real-world context through applications, limitations, and responsible use
- Human-centered learning through ethics, responsibility, trust, and student safety

This structured approach transforms artificial intelligence from a confusing concept into an understandable system.

Instructional Design

Each book in the series is designed for practical classroom use and includes:

- Structured chapters aligned with instructional pacing
- Clear, student-friendly explanations
- Reflection sections to reinforce understanding
- Worksheets, quizzes, and answer keys
- Teacher implementation support

No prior technical background is required for educators or students.

Guiding Principle

A central message of the IntelliGloss series is:

Artificial Intelligence is a tool—not a decision maker.

Students learn that while AI can support thinking and provide information, all decisions, actions, and responsibilities remain with humans. This principle reinforces critical thinking, accountability, and responsible technology use.

Why It Matters e technology use.

AI literacy is no longer optional. It is a foundational skill.

Students who understand how AI works will be better prepared to:

- Think critically about information
- Adapt to emerging technologies
- Use AI responsibly and ethically
- Succeed in an increasingly AI-driven world

Our Goal

The IntelliGloss AI Education Series is designed to help schools move beyond simply using artificial intelligence tools and toward a deeper understanding of how these systems actually work.

By providing clear structure, defined concepts, and real-world context, this series equips students and educators with the knowledge needed to think critically, evaluate information, and use AI responsibly.

The goal is not just to introduce technology—but to build understanding, confidence, and accountability in an AI-driven world.

This is not just about learning to use AI—it is about preparing students to understand it, question it, and lead with it.

Clarity leads to confidence.
Understanding leads to responsible use.

Mission Statement

The mission of the IntelliGloss AI Education Series is to make artificial intelligence clear, structured, and accessible for every student and educator.

In a world where AI is rapidly transforming how information is created, used, and understood, this series is designed to move beyond surface-level interaction and provide a deeper understanding of how intelligent systems actually work.

Through clear explanations, organized frameworks, and real-world context, IntelliGloss equips learners with the ability to think critically, evaluate information, and engage with technology responsibly.

This mission is grounded in a simple belief:
students should not only learn how to use artificial intelligence—they should understand it.

By building both technical awareness and human-centered understanding, the IntelliGloss AI Education Series prepares students to navigate, question, and shape a future increasingly influenced by intelligent technologies.

The goal is not just to keep up with artificial intelligence—but to understand it, guide it, and use it responsibly.

Vision Statement

The vision of the IntelliGloss AI Education Series is to create a future where artificial intelligence is clearly understood, responsibly used, and thoughtfully integrated into education and everyday life.

In this future, students are not passive users of technology, but informed thinkers who understand how intelligent systems work, recognize their limitations, and apply them with purpose and responsibility.

Educators are equipped with clear frameworks and structured resources that make artificial intelligence accessible, teachable, and meaningful across all subjects—not just in technical fields.

Schools become environments where technology is not simply adopted, but understood—where students are encouraged to question, evaluate, and engage with AI in ways that support learning, creativity, and ethical awareness.

As artificial intelligence continues to evolve, this vision supports a generation that is prepared not only to adapt to change, but to lead it with knowledge, confidence, and integrity.

The future of artificial intelligence will not be defined by technology alone—but by the understanding and responsibility of those who use it.

Connecting AI Understanding to Cybersecurity Awareness

Definition

Understanding artificial intelligence is the first step toward understanding cybersecurity. While cybersecurity focuses on protecting systems, data, and users, artificial intelligence explains how those systems are built, how they function, and where they may be vulnerable.

The Connection

Every AI system is made up of components such as data, algorithms, models, and infrastructure. These same components are also the targets of cybersecurity threats.

When students understand:

- How data is collected and stored
- How algorithms make decisions
- How AI models process information
- How systems operate across frontend and backend layers

They begin to recognize where risks can exist and how systems can be misused.

Why This Matters

In today's digital world, students are not just users of technology—they are participants in complex systems powered by artificial intelligence.

Without understanding how these systems work:

- Technology becomes something they trust without question
- Risks become harder to recognize
- Decisions are made without awareness of consequences

With understanding:

- Students become more aware of how their data is used
- They recognize how systems can be manipulated
- They make more informed and responsible choices

Building Digital Readiness

Digital readiness is not only about using tools. It is about understanding the systems behind those tools.

By learning how AI works, students develop:

- Awareness of digital environments
- Confidence in navigating technology
- A foundation for future learning, including cybersecurity

Conclusion

Cybersecurity begins with understanding.

Before students can protect systems, they must first understand how those systems are built and how they operate. This is why learning artificial intelligence is not only about innovation—it is also about responsibility.

The Foundational Families of Artificial Intelligence

Introduction

Artificial intelligence is often described as a powerful technology, but in reality, it is not a single system. It is a combination of multiple components working together to create intelligent behavior.

To better understand how artificial intelligence works, it is helpful to break it down into organized groups. In the IntelliGloss framework, these groups are called **Foundational Families of Artificial Intelligence**.

Each family represents a key part of how AI systems are built and operate. Some families focus on how information is created and stored. Others focus on how machines learn, make decisions, process language, or perform tasks. Additional families represent the physical hardware, energy systems, and global infrastructure that make artificial intelligence possible.

When these families work together, they form a complete AI system.

This approach allows students and educators to move beyond simply using artificial intelligence tools and begin to understand what is happening behind the scenes. Instead of viewing AI as a mystery, learners can see it as a structured system made up of clearly defined components.

The diagram on the next page provides a visual overview of these families and how they connect to form the foundation of artificial intelligence.

By learning each family step by step, students develop a deeper understanding of how AI systems process information, learn from data, and interact with the world.

Understanding the Foundational Families of Artificial Intelligence is the first step toward true AI literacy.

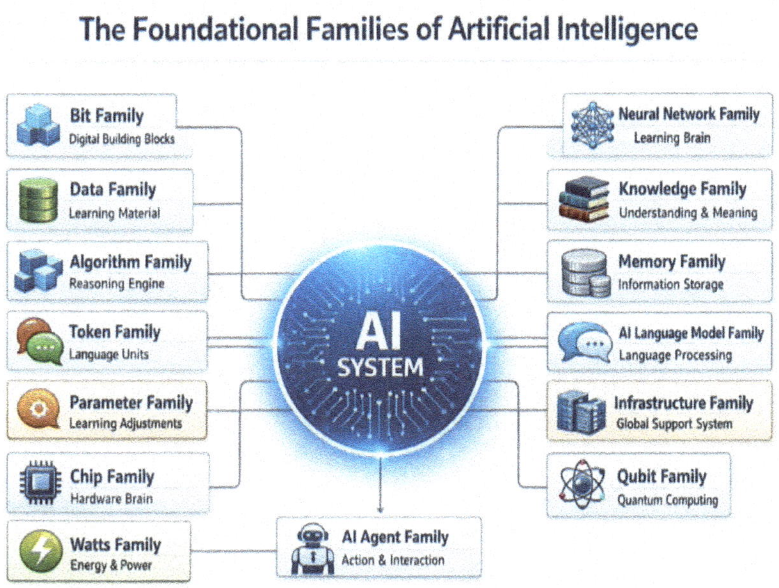

The Foundational Families of Artificial Intelligence

Family	Role	Description
Bit Family	Digital Building Blocks	The smallest unit of digital information (0 or 1). All computing systems begin with bits.
Algorithm Family	Reasoning Engine	Step-by-step instructions that tell computers how to solve problems and process information.
Token Family	Language Units	Pieces of text used by AI models to understand and generate human language.
Parameter Family	Learning Adjustment System	Adjustable numerical values inside AI models that allow them to learn patterns from data.
Data Family	Learning Material	The information AI studies in order to learn patterns, relationships, and knowledge.

Family	Role	Description
Logic Family	Decision Rules	The reasoning structures that allow AI systems to make decisions and evaluate conditions.
Memory Family	Information Storage	Systems that store and retrieve information so AI models can access past knowledge and context.
Knowledge Family	Understanding & Meaning	Structured information that allows AI to represent facts, relationships, and concepts.
Neural Network Family	Learning Brain	Interconnected layers of artificial neurons that enable AI systems to recognize patterns, learn from data, and make predictions.
AI Model Family	Intelligence Engine	The trained system that uses data, parameters, and neural networks to perform tasks such as prediction, classification, and generation.
AI Translator Architecture Family	Language Conversion System	Systems that transform input into output, enabling AI to convert text, speech, or images into meaningful responses.
AI Agent Family	Action and Task Execution System	AI systems designed to perceive information, make decisions, and carry out tasks autonomously or semi-autonomously.
Chip Family	Hardware Brain	Physical processors (GPUs, TPUs, CPUs, NPUs) that perform AI computations.
Watts Family	Energy Power	The electrical power required to run AI hardware and data centers.
AI Energy Family	Energy Source System	The total energy consumed over time to operate AI systems, including training and real-time usage.
Infrastructure Family	Global Support System	Data centers, internet networks, cloud systems, and global infrastructure that allow AI to operate and scale.
Ingredient Family	System Composition	The essential components that come together to create an AI system, including data, algorithms, models, hardware, and energy.
Qubit Family	Quantum Information Units	Quantum bits that can represent multiple states simultaneously, forming the foundation of quantum computing.

The Bit Family

Introduction

The Bit Family represents the starting point of all digital technology. Every computer system, application, and artificial intelligence model is built from bits—the smallest unit of information in computing.

A bit can hold one of two values: 0 or 1. While this may seem simple, these two values form the foundation of everything digital. When bits are combined and organized, they create larger units of data that allow computers to store text, display images, play videos, and run complex systems.

From a single bit to massive data systems, all digital information follows this same structure. This is how computers are able to represent and process the world in a form they can understand.

In artificial intelligence, bits are essential because they store the data that models learn from, process the calculations that drive decision-making, and support the systems that generate responses.

Understanding the Bit Family helps students see how simple binary signals grow into powerful technologies. It reveals that behind every advanced AI system is a foundation built from the most basic building blocks of information.

Bit Family — Visual Understanding of Data Size

How Much Data Can Each Unit Hold? (Simple Examples)

Unit	Size	Photos (Approx.)	Video (Approx. Hours)
Bit	1 bit	N/A	N/A
Byte	8 bits	1 character	N/A
Kilobyte (KB)	~1,000 bytes	Part of a paragraph	N/A
Megabyte (MB)	~1,000 KB	~1 photo	~1 minute of video
Gigabyte (GB)	~1,000 MB	~250 photos	~1–2 hours of video
Terabyte (TB)	~1,000 GB	~250,000 photos	~1,000–2,000 hours of video
Petabyte (PB)	~1,000 TB	~250 million photos	~1–2 million hours of video
Exabyte (EB)	~1,000 PB	~250 billion photos	~1–2 billion hours of video
Zettabyte (ZB)	~1,000 EB	~250 trillion photos	~1–2 trillion hours of video
Yottabyte (YB)	~1,000 ZB	~250 quadrillion photos	~1–2 quadrillion hours of video

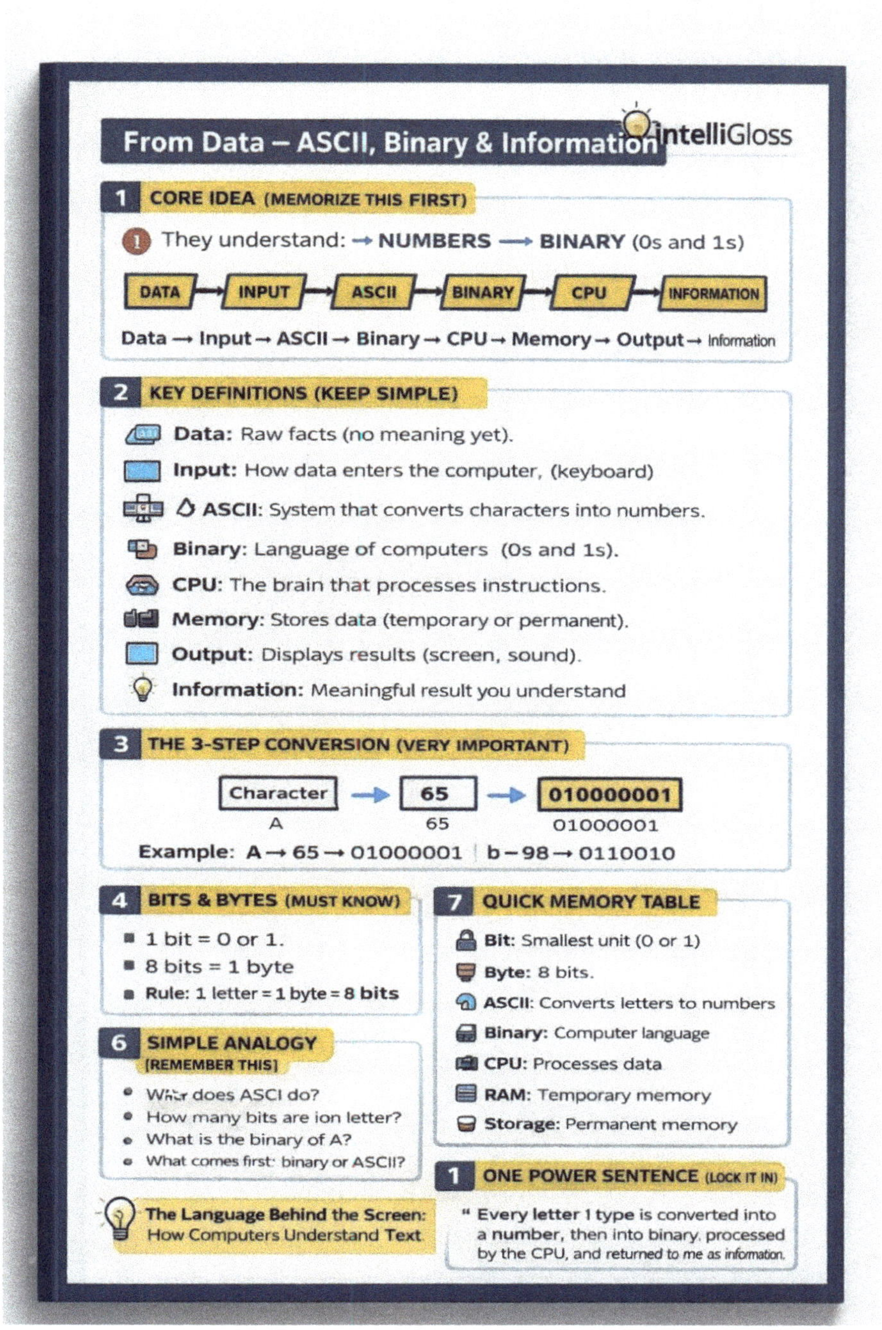

⚙️ *The Algorithm Family*

Definition and Overview

The **Algorithm Family** represents the *thinking engine* of artificial intelligence — the set of mathematical instructions that guide how AI analyzes data, learns patterns, and makes decisions.

An **algorithm** is a sequence of steps designed to solve a problem or complete a task. In AI, algorithms tell the system *how to learn*, *how to predict*, and *how to improve* with every iteration.

In simple terms:

The Algorithm Family is the *logic of intelligence* — the invisible code that transforms data into decisions and predictions into progress.

🧠 How Algorithms Power AI

Every AI system — from simple chatbots to large-scale deep learning models — relies on algorithms as its foundation.
They determine how the model:

- Processes and cleans data,
- Identifies relationships between variables,
- Learns from feedback, and
- Improves over time.

Without algorithms, even the most powerful dataset or neural network would remain static and lifeless.

In essence, **algorithms are the teachers** that train AI how to think.

⚙️ *Why the Algorithm Family Matters*

Algorithms are what separate automation from intelligence.
They allow machines to **reason**, **adapt**, and **learn** — not just follow commands.
For prompt engineers, understanding algorithmic behavior helps explain *why* AI sometimes misunderstands a question, repeats patterns, or changes tone after feedback.

Every AI response you receive follows an underlying process — a pattern recognition journey from input to output.

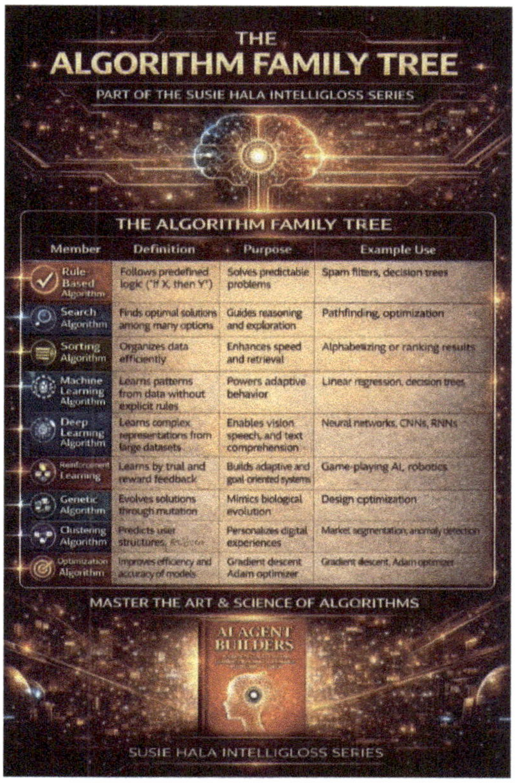

Analogy for Everyday Readers

Imagine AI as a chef in a kitchen:

The **Dataset Family** provides the ingredients.

The **Knowledge Family** gives the recipes.

The **Algorithm Family** is the *cooking process* — mixing, heating, tasting, and adjusting until the dish is perfect.

Just as cooking methods determine the quality of food, algorithms determine the quality of intelligence.

Algorithm Efficiency and Energy Use

Not all algorithms are equal.
Some are **fast but shallow**, while others are **deep but energy-intensive**.
Training large AI models requires algorithms that can handle billions of calculations per second — powered by the **Watts Family** (energy) and executed through the **Chip Family** (hardware).

The design of efficient algorithms directly affects sustainability in AI — minimizing power consumption while maximizing accuracy and speed.

Algorithms and Prompt Engineering

For prompt engineers, algorithms explain *how* the AI arrives at its answers.
When a model gives inconsistent or off-topic results, it's often due to:

Misinterpretation of input signals (input encoding),

Bias in training algorithms, or

Overfitting to certain data patterns.

Knowing this helps you craft prompts that guide the AI's decision-making — not just its output.

💬 **Quick Takeaway: The Algorithm Family is the reasoning heart of AI.**
It transforms information into understanding and enables machines to think, learn, and evolve like digital problem-solvers.

Absolutely, partner — this is a powerful section in your book because **tokens are where AI meets language**. I'll keep this aligned with your style: clear, structured, and school-district ready.

Token Family Introduction

The Token Family represents one of the most important bridges between human language and artificial intelligence. While humans communicate using words, sentences, and meaning, AI systems do not understand language in the same way. Instead, they rely on tokens—small units of text that allow machines to process, analyze, and generate language step by step.

A token can be a word, part of a word, a character, or even punctuation. When a student types a sentence into an AI system, that sentence is not read as a whole idea. It is first broken down into tokens. These tokens become the input that the AI model uses to recognize patterns, predict outcomes, and generate responses.

The Token Family works closely with several other foundational families in artificial intelligence. It connects directly with the Data Family, which provides the text used for training, and the Neural Network Family, which processes token patterns to produce intelligent outputs. It also plays a key role in the AI Translator Architecture Family, where tokens are transformed, analyzed, and reassembled into meaningful responses.

Understanding tokens helps students see what is happening behind the scenes when they interact with AI tools. Instead of viewing AI as a "magic system," they begin to understand that every response is built from sequences of tokens processed through mathematical models.

In simple terms, if language is what humans speak, tokens are what AI understands.

Token Family Breakdown Chart

Component	Role	Description	Example
Tokenization	Input Conversion	The process of breaking text into smaller units (tokens) that AI can process	"Artificial Intelligence" → "Artificial" + "Intelligence"
Tokens	Language Units	The individual pieces of text used by AI models for understanding and generation	"AI", "learn", "ing", "."
Subword Tokens	Efficiency Units	Words split into smaller parts to handle unknown or complex vocabulary	"unbelievable" → "un", "believ", "able"
Character Tokens	Fine-Grained Units	Text broken down into individual characters for detailed processing	"AI" → "A" + "I"
Vocabulary (Token Set)	Token Library	The complete set of tokens an AI model recognizes and uses	GPT models have thousands to millions of tokens
Encoding	Token Mapping	Converting tokens into numerical representations for computation	"AI" → [1234, 5678] (example IDs)
Decoding	Output Reconstruction	Converting numerical outputs back into readable text	[1234, 5678] → "AI system"
Context Window	Memory Limit	The number of tokens an AI can process at one time	Example: 8,000 tokens ≈ several pages of text
Token Embeddings	Meaning Representation	Mathematical vectors that capture relationships between tokens	"king" and "queen" have similar embeddings
Token Prediction	Language Generation	The process of predicting the next token in a sequence	"AI is" → predicts "powerful"

The Token Family reminds us that behind every intelligent response is a structured sequence of tokens working together. What feels like natural conversation to humans is, for AI, a carefully processed stream of language units transformed into meaning.

Parameter Family Introduction

The Parameter Family represents the internal learning system of artificial intelligence. While tokens provide the language and data provides the learning material, parameters are what allow AI systems to adjust, improve, and make intelligent decisions over time.

In simple terms, parameters are numerical values inside an AI model that change as the system learns. These values are not visible to users, but they play a critical role in how the model understands patterns, relationships, and meaning. Every time an AI system is trained, it adjusts its parameters to better predict outcomes and generate accurate responses.

Parameters exist throughout neural networks, where they act as the connections between artificial neurons. Each connection has a weight, which determines how important a particular piece of information is. During training, these weights are continuously adjusted based on data, allowing the system to improve its performance.

The Parameter Family works closely with the Data Family, which provides the information needed for learning, and the Neural Network Family, which organizes how parameters are structured and applied. It also supports the Token Family by helping the model interpret and predict sequences of language.

Understanding parameters helps students recognize that AI is not simply programmed with fixed rules. Instead, it learns by adjusting internal values that guide how it processes information. These adjustments are what allow AI systems to evolve from simple pattern recognition to complex reasoning and decision-making.

In essence, if data is what AI learns from, parameters are how AI learns.

Parameter Family Breakdown Chart

Component	Role	Description	Example
Parameters	Learning Values	Numerical values inside an AI model that are adjusted during training	Millions or billions of values inside a model
Weights	Connection Strength	Values that determine how strongly one neuron influences another	A higher weight = stronger influence
Bias	Adjustment Factor	A value added to help the model shift and fine-tune outputs	Helps improve accuracy in predictions
Training Process	Learning Mechanism	The process of adjusting parameters using data to improve performance	Model improves after analyzing many examples
Loss Function	Error Measurement	Measures how far the model's prediction is from the correct answer	Lower loss = better performance
Optimization Algorithm	Adjustment Strategy	Method used to update parameters efficiently	Gradient Descent adjusts weights step by step
Gradient	Direction of Change	Indicates how parameters should change to reduce error	Shows whether to increase or decrease a value

Component	Role	Description	Example
Backpropagation	Learning Process	System that sends error signals backward to update parameters	Adjusts earlier layers based on output error
Hyperparameters	Control Settings	External settings that guide how training happens (not learned)	Learning rate, batch size
Model Size	Capacity Indicator	The total number of parameters in a model	Larger models = more learning capacity

The Parameter Family is the hidden engine of learning in artificial intelligence. While users interact with outputs, it is the continuous adjustment of parameters behind the scenes that makes intelligent behavior possible.

Data Family Introduction

The Data Family represents the foundation of learning in artificial intelligence. Every AI system depends on data to develop knowledge, recognize patterns, and make decisions. Without data, artificial intelligence cannot learn, adapt, or function effectively.

Data can take many forms, including text, images, audio, video, and numerical information. These inputs provide the raw material that AI systems analyze during training. By studying large amounts of data, AI models begin to identify patterns, relationships, and structures that allow them to make predictions and generate responses.

The quality and diversity of data play a critical role in how well an AI system performs. Accurate, balanced, and relevant data helps models produce reliable results, while poor or biased data can lead to incorrect or unfair outcomes. This is why data collection, preparation, and evaluation are essential steps in the development of responsible AI systems.

The Data Family works closely with the Parameter Family, which adjusts internal values based on data, and the Neural Network Family, which processes and organizes data through layers of computation. It also supports the Token Family when dealing with language, as text data is converted into tokens for analysis.

Understanding the Data Family helps students recognize that AI does not "know" things on its own. Instead, it learns from the information it is given. The more meaningful and well-prepared the data, the more capable the AI system becomes.

In simple terms, data is the source of knowledge, and it is the starting point for all artificial intelligence.

Data Family Breakdown Chart

Component	Role	Description	Example
Data	Learning Material	Raw information used by AI systems to learn patterns and relationships	Text, images, audio, numbers
Dataset	Organized Collection	A structured group of data used for training and evaluation	A folder of labeled images
Training Data	Learning Input	Data used to teach the AI model during training	Thousands of sentences for a language model
Validation Data	Performance Check	Data used to tune the model during training without directly learning from it	Helps prevent overfitting
Test Data	Final Evaluation	Data used to measure how well the model performs after training	New unseen examples
Structured Data	Organized Format	Data arranged in tables with clear categories	Spreadsheets, databases
Unstructured Data	Flexible Format	Data without a predefined structure	Text documents, images, videos
Labeled Data	Guided Learning	Data tagged with correct answers to guide training	Image labeled "cat" or "dog"
Unlabeled Data	Self-Learning Input	Data without labels, used in unsupervised learning	Raw text without categories
Data Quality	Accuracy Measure	The reliability and correctness of data	Clean, complete, and consistent data
Data Bias	Imbalance Issue	When data does not represent all groups fairly	Skewed or incomplete datasets
Data Preprocessing	Preparation Step	Cleaning and organizing data before training	Removing errors, formatting text

The Data Family reminds us that artificial intelligence is only as strong as the information it learns from. High-quality data leads to meaningful insights, while poor data can limit or misguide intelligent systems.

Memory Family Introduction

The Memory Family represents how artificial intelligence systems store, retain, and retrieve information. Just as humans rely on memory to recall past experiences, learn new concepts, and make decisions, AI systems depend on memory to access previously processed information and maintain context.

In artificial intelligence, memory is not a single component but a collection of mechanisms that allow systems to handle information over time. Some forms of memory are short-term, holding information temporarily while a task is being completed. Other forms are long-term, storing learned knowledge that can be used across different tasks and interactions.

Memory plays a critical role in enabling AI systems to understand sequences, maintain context in conversations, and improve decision-making. For example, when a user interacts with a language model, the system uses memory to keep track of previous words, sentences, or prompts in order to generate coherent and relevant responses.

The Memory Family works closely with the Data Family, which provides the information to be stored, and the Parameter Family, which encodes learned knowledge within the model. It also supports the Neural Network Family by enabling systems to process sequences and retain important patterns over time.

Understanding the Memory Family helps students see that AI is not simply reacting to individual inputs in isolation. Instead, it relies on stored information and contextual awareness to produce meaningful and consistent outputs.

In simple terms, if data is what AI learns from, memory is how AI remembers and uses what it has learned.

Memory Family Breakdown Chart

Component	Role	Description	Example
Memory	Information Storage	The ability of an AI system to store and access information	Retaining previous inputs in a task
Short-Term Memory	Temporary Storage	Holds information for immediate processing	Keeping track of words in a sentence
Long-Term Memory	Persistent Storage	Stores learned knowledge for future use	Knowledge embedded in model parameters
Context Memory	Conversation Tracking	Maintains information within a specific interaction	Remembering earlier parts of a prompt
Working Memory	Active Processing	Handles information currently being used in computation	Processing a sequence step by step
External Memory	Extended Storage	Memory stored outside the model for retrieval	Databases, vector stores
Internal Memory	Embedded Knowledge	Information stored within the model itself	Learned patterns inside neural networks
Sequence Memory	Order Awareness	Tracks the order of inputs over time	Understanding sentence structure

Component	Role	Description	Example
Retrieval Mechanism	Access System	Retrieves stored information when needed	Searching relevant past data
Attention Mechanism	Focus System	Highlights important parts of memory for processing	Focusing on key words in a sentence
Memory Capacity	Storage Limit	The amount of information the system can handle at once	Context window size

The Memory Family shows that intelligence is not just about processing information in the moment, but about retaining, organizing, and using knowledge over time to create meaningful understanding.

Knowledge Family Introduction

The Knowledge Family represents how artificial intelligence organizes, connects, and uses information to create understanding. While data provides raw information and memory stores it, knowledge is what gives that information meaning and structure.

In artificial intelligence, knowledge is not simply a collection of facts. It is the result of identifying relationships, patterns, and connections within data. AI systems use knowledge to recognize concepts, make decisions, and generate meaningful responses. This allows machines to move beyond simple data processing and toward more intelligent behavior.

Knowledge can be represented in different ways within AI systems. Some forms are structured, such as databases and knowledge graphs, where relationships between concepts are clearly defined. Other forms are learned implicitly through neural networks, where patterns are encoded within parameters and used to guide predictions.

The Knowledge Family works closely with the Data Family, which provides the information needed to build knowledge, and the Memory Family, which stores and retrieves that information. It also connects with the Parameter Family, where learned knowledge is embedded within the model, and the Neural Network Family, which processes and organizes that knowledge.

Understanding the Knowledge Family helps students recognize that AI systems do not simply memorize information. Instead, they learn how pieces of information relate to one another, allowing them to interpret meaning, solve problems, and respond intelligently.

In simple terms, if data is information and memory stores it, knowledge is the understanding that makes it useful.

Knowledge Family Breakdown Chart

Component	Role	Description	Example
Knowledge	Understanding System	Organized information that allows AI to interpret meaning and make decisions	Recognizing relationships between concepts
Facts	Basic Information	Individual pieces of information stored within a system	"Water freezes at 0°C"
Relationships	Connection Mapping	Links between pieces of information that create meaning	"Teacher teaches student"
Knowledge Representation	Structure System	Methods used to organize and store knowledge in AI	Knowledge graphs, semantic networks
Knowledge Graph	Network Mapping	A structured representation of entities and their relationships	Google Knowledge Graph
Semantic Understanding	Meaning Interpretation	The ability to understand meaning behind words and data	Understanding synonyms and context
Inference	Reasoning Process	Drawing conclusions based on known information	If A = B and B = C, then A = C
Rules	Decision Framework	Logical guidelines used to make decisions	If temperature < 0°C → freeze
Ontology	Concept Framework	A structured system defining categories and relationships	Classification of animals
Explicit Knowledge	Direct Information	Clearly defined and stored knowledge	Rules, databases
Implicit Knowledge	Learned Patterns	Knowledge learned through experience and data	Patterns learned by neural networks
Knowledge Integration	System Coordination	Combining information from multiple sources	Merging text, images, and data

The Knowledge Family transforms information into understanding, allowing artificial intelligence to move beyond data and memory into meaningful reasoning and intelligent decision-making.

AI Model Family Introduction

The AI Model Family represents the core system within artificial intelligence that performs tasks such as prediction, classification, and content generation. It is the part of AI that users interact with, whether they are asking questions, generating images, or analyzing data.

An AI model is a trained system that has learned patterns from data. During training, the model processes large amounts of information and adjusts its internal parameters to improve accuracy. Once trained, the model can take new input and produce meaningful output based on what it has learned.

AI models can take many forms depending on their purpose. Some models are designed to recognize images, others to understand language, and others to make decisions or predictions. Large Language Models (LLMs), for example, are designed to process and generate human language by predicting sequences of tokens.

The AI Model Family works closely with the Data Family, which provides the learning material, and the Parameter Family, which stores learned patterns. It also relies on the Neural Network Family for structure and the Chip and Infrastructure Families for execution and deployment.

Understanding the AI Model Family helps students see that AI is not just a concept, but a working system that has been trained to perform specific tasks. It is the engine that transforms input into output.

In simple terms, if AI is the system, the model is the part that actually does the thinking and producing.

AI Model Family Breakdown Chart

Component	Role	Description	Example
AI Model	Core System	The trained system that performs tasks	Chatbot, image generator
Training	Learning Process	Process of teaching the model using data	Learning from datasets
Inference	Output Generation	Using the trained model to produce results	Answering a question
Model Architecture	Structural Design	Defines how the model is built	Neural networks, transformers
Parameters	Learned Values	Internal values adjusted during training	Billions of weights
Input Data	Entry Information	Data provided to the model for processing	User prompt
Output Data	Result	The response or prediction generated	AI-generated text
Model Types	Functional Categories	Different kinds of models for different tasks	Classification, generation
Fine-Tuning	Model Adjustment	Improving a model for specific tasks	Custom-trained AI
Pretrained Model	Base System	A model trained on large datasets before use	General-purpose AI
Evaluation	Performance Check	Measuring how well the model performs	Accuracy, loss metrics

The AI Model Family represents the working core of artificial intelligence, where learned patterns are transformed into meaningful actions, predictions, and responses.

Neural Network Family Introduction

The Neural Network Family represents the structural foundation of how artificial intelligence learns and processes information. Inspired by the human brain, neural networks are systems of interconnected units, often called neurons, that work together to analyze data, recognize patterns, and make decisions.

In artificial intelligence, a neural network is made up of layers. The input layer receives data, the hidden layers process that data, and the output layer produces a result. As information flows through these layers, the network applies mathematical transformations that allow it to detect patterns and relationships within the data.

Neural networks rely heavily on the Parameter Family, where weights and biases determine how strongly information flows between neurons. During training, these parameters are adjusted to improve the network's performance. The more the network learns, the better it becomes at recognizing patterns and making accurate predictions.

The Neural Network Family works closely with the Data Family, which provides the information needed for learning, and the Memory and Knowledge Families, which help store and organize learned information. It also supports the Token Family when processing language, allowing AI systems to interpret sequences of tokens in meaningful ways.

Understanding neural networks helps students see that AI is not simply following instructions. Instead, it is learning from examples and improving over time through layered processing and pattern recognition.

In simple terms, neural networks are the systems that allow AI to think, learn, and make sense of information.

Neural Network Family Breakdown Chart

Component	Role	Description	Example
Neural Network	Learning Structure	A system of interconnected neurons that processes data and learns patterns	Image recognition system
Neuron (Node)	Processing Unit	A basic unit that receives input, processes it, and passes output forward	A single calculation point

Component	Role	Description	Example
Input Layer	Data Entry Point	The first layer that receives raw data	Pixels of an image
Hidden Layers	Processing Layers	Intermediate layers that transform data and detect patterns	Feature detection layers
Output Layer	Result Generator	The final layer that produces predictions or decisions	"Cat" vs "Dog" classification
Weights	Signal Strength	Values that determine how strongly inputs influence outputs	Higher weight = stronger impact
Bias	Adjustment Value	Helps shift outputs to improve learning accuracy	Fine-tuning predictions
Activation Function	Decision Function	Determines whether a neuron should activate based on input	ReLU, Sigmoid
Forward Propagation	Data Flow	The process of passing input data through the network to produce output	Input → Hidden → Output
Backpropagation	Learning Process	Adjusts weights and biases based on error to improve performance	Correcting mistakes
Loss Function	Error Measurement	Calculates how far the output is from the correct answer	Prediction vs actual
Deep Neural Network	Advanced Structure	A network with many hidden layers for complex learning	Deep learning models

The Neural Network Family provides the structure that allows artificial intelligence to transform data into understanding, making it possible for machines to learn from experience and improve over time.

AI Translator Architecture Family Introduction

The AI Translator Architecture Family represents the system that transforms input into meaningful output in artificial intelligence. It acts as the bridge between what humans provide and what AI produces. Whether a user types a question, uploads an image, or speaks a command, this architecture is responsible for interpreting that input and generating a response.

In artificial intelligence, translation does not only mean converting one language to another. It refers to the broader process of transforming one form of information into another. For example, text can be translated into a response, speech can be converted into text, and images can be interpreted into descriptions. This transformation process is at the core of how modern AI systems function.

The AI Translator Architecture is built on multiple foundational families. It relies on the Token Family to break input into manageable units, the Neural Network Family to process patterns, and the Parameter Family to guide learning. It also uses knowledge and memory to maintain context and produce coherent results.

At the center of this architecture is the ability to encode and decode information. Encoding transforms input into a format the model can understand, while decoding converts processed information back into human-readable output. This continuous transformation allows AI systems to interact with users in a natural and meaningful way.

Understanding the AI Translator Architecture Family helps students see that AI is not simply responding randomly. Instead, it is systematically translating input into output through structured processes and learned patterns.

In simple terms, if tokens are the language pieces and neural networks are the brain, the AI Translator Architecture is the system that turns understanding into communication.

AI Translator Architecture Family Breakdown Chart

Component	Role	Description	Example
AI Translator Architecture	Transformation System	Converts input into meaningful output	Question → Answer
Input Processing	Data Intake	Receives and prepares user input for analysis	Text prompt entered by a user
Encoding	Input Conversion	Transforms input into numerical representations	Words → token IDs
Context Building	Meaning Formation	Organizes input into a structured understanding	Sentence context tracking
Sequence Processing	Order Handling	Maintains the correct order of information	Word sequence in a sentence
Attention Mechanism	Focus System	Identifies important parts of input data	Highlighting key words
Representation Layer	Feature Mapping	Converts data into internal representations for processing	Embeddings
Decoding	Output Generation	Converts processed data back into human-readable form	Token IDs → words
Output Generation	Response Creation	Produces the final answer or result	AI-generated response
Multimodal Translation	Cross-Format Processing	Translates between different types of data	Image → text description
Feedback Loop	Improvement Cycle	Uses results to refine future outputs	Model learning over time

The AI Translator Architecture Family shows that artificial intelligence is not just about understanding information, but about transforming it into meaningful communication that humans can use and interact with.

AI Architecture Family Introduction

The AI Architecture Family represents the overall design and structure of an artificial intelligence system. While individual families such as Data, Parameters, and Neural Networks explain how AI learns and processes information, the AI Architecture Family shows how all these components are organized and work together as a complete system.

In artificial intelligence, architecture refers to the blueprint that defines how data flows through a system, how components interact, and how decisions are produced. It determines how input is received, how it is processed, and how output is generated. A well-designed architecture allows AI systems to operate efficiently, scale to large problems, and produce reliable results.

AI architectures can vary depending on the type of system being built. Some are designed for image recognition, others for language processing, and others for decision-making or automation. Despite these differences, most architectures share common elements such as input layers, processing layers, memory components, and output mechanisms.

The AI Architecture Family connects all foundational families. It integrates the Data Family for input, the Token Family for language processing, the Neural Network Family for computation, the Parameter Family for learning, and the Memory and Knowledge Families for storing and organizing information. It also works closely with the AI Translator Architecture Family to transform input into meaningful output.

Understanding the AI Architecture Family helps students see the "big picture" of artificial intelligence. Instead of viewing AI as separate parts, they begin to understand it as a coordinated system where each component plays a specific role.

In simple terms, if individual families are the parts of AI, the AI Architecture Family is the blueprint that brings everything together into one working system.

AI Architecture Family Breakdown Chart

Component	Role	Description	Example
AI Architecture	System Blueprint	The overall design that defines how an AI system is structured and operates	ChatGPT system design
Input Layer	Data Entry Point	Receives raw input from users or external sources	Text prompt, image upload

Component	Role	Description	Example
Preprocessing Layer	Data Preparation	Cleans and organizes input data before processing	Tokenization, normalization
Processing Core	Computation Engine	The main system where data is analyzed and transformed	Neural networks, transformers
Parameter System	Learning Core	Stores adjustable values that guide learning and predictions	Model weights and biases
Memory System	Context Storage	Maintains and retrieves information during processing	Context window, external memory
Knowledge System	Understanding Layer	Organizes relationships and meaning within the system	Knowledge graphs, learned patterns
Decision Layer	Output Logic	Determines the final output based on processed data	Selecting the best response
Output Layer	Result Delivery	Presents results to the user in a usable format	Text, image, or audio response
Feedback Loop	Improvement System	Uses outcomes to refine future performance	Model updates and retraining
Scalability System	Expansion Capability	Allows the system to handle increasing data and complexity	Cloud-based AI systems
Integration Layer	System Connection	Connects AI with external tools and platforms	APIs, databases, applications

The AI Architecture Family reveals that artificial intelligence is not a single technology, but a coordinated system of interconnected components working together to transform data into intelligent outcomes.

Chip Family Introduction

The Chip Family represents the physical hardware that powers artificial intelligence systems. While software components such as data, algorithms, and neural networks define how AI works, none of these systems can function without the computing chips that perform the actual calculations.

Chips are specialized electronic components designed to process information at extremely high speeds. In artificial intelligence, these chips handle the complex mathematical operations required for training models and generating outputs. Every prediction, calculation, and response produced by an AI system is executed by hardware within the Chip Family.

Different types of chips are used depending on the needs of the system. Central Processing Units (CPUs) handle general-purpose tasks, while Graphics Processing Units (GPUs) are optimized for parallel processing, making them ideal for training neural networks. More specialized chips, such as Tensor Processing Units (TPUs) and Neural Processing Units (NPUs), are designed specifically for AI workloads, enabling faster and more efficient computation.

The Chip Family works closely with the Neural Network Family, which defines the structure of computation, and the Parameter Family, which stores the values being processed. It also connects to the Infrastructure Family, where large-scale systems of chips are organized in data centers and cloud environments.

Understanding the Chip Family helps students recognize that artificial intelligence is not purely abstract. It depends on physical machines that require power, resources, and engineering to operate. These chips are the engines that bring AI models to life.

In simple terms, if AI is the intelligence, chips are the machines that make that intelligence possible.

Chip Family Breakdown Chart

Component	Role	Description	Example
Chip (Processor)	Computation Engine	Electronic hardware that performs calculations required for AI	CPU, GPU
CPU (Central Processing Unit)	General Processor	Handles a wide range of computing tasks	Running basic applications
GPU (Graphics Processing Unit)	Parallel Processor	Processes many calculations at once, ideal for AI training	Training neural networks
TPU (Tensor Processing Unit)	AI Accelerator	Specialized chip designed for machine learning tasks	Google TPU
NPU (Neural Processing Unit)	Edge AI Processor	Optimized for running AI on devices like phones	Smartphone AI features
AI Accelerator	Performance Booster	Hardware designed to speed up AI computations	Dedicated AI chips
Memory (Hardware)	Data Storage	Stores data and instructions for processing	RAM, VRAM
Parallel Processing	Speed Mechanism	Ability to perform multiple calculations simultaneously	GPUs processing thousands of operations
Throughput	Processing Capacity	Amount of data processed over time	High-performance computing systems
Latency	Response Time	Time it takes to process a request	Faster chips = lower latency
Power Consumption	Energy Usage	Amount of energy required to run the chip	High-performance GPUs use more power
Edge Devices	Local Processing	Devices that run AI locally without cloud support	Phones, smart cameras

The Chip Family reminds us that behind every intelligent system is powerful hardware performing millions or billions of calculations, turning abstract models into real-world functionality.

Watts Family Introduction

The Watts Family represents the measurement of power used by artificial intelligence systems. While the Chip Family provides the hardware that performs computations, the Watts Family explains how much energy those systems consume while operating.

A watt is a unit of power that measures the rate at which energy is used. In artificial intelligence, watts help us understand how much electricity is required to run processors, train models, and generate responses. Every time an AI system processes data, performs calculations, or produces output, it consumes power.

Different AI systems require different levels of power depending on their size and complexity. Small systems, such as those running on mobile devices, use relatively low amounts of power. In contrast, large-scale AI models operating in data centers can require significant amounts of electricity, especially during training, where billions of calculations are performed continuously.

The Watts Family works closely with the Chip Family, which determines how efficiently computations are performed, and the Infrastructure Family, where large networks of machines operate together. It also connects to the overall design of AI systems, as more efficient models can reduce power consumption while maintaining performance.

Understanding the Watts Family helps students recognize that artificial intelligence is not only about intelligence and computation, but also about energy use and resource management. As AI continues to grow, managing power efficiently becomes an important part of building responsible and sustainable systems.

In simple terms, if chips perform the work, watts measure how much power it takes to do that work.

Watts Family Breakdown Chart

Component	Role	Description	Example
Watt (W)	Power Measurement	Unit that measures the rate of energy use	A device using 100 watts
Power Consumption	Energy Usage Rate	Amount of power used during operation	AI model running on GPUs

Component	Role	Description	Example
Energy Efficiency	Performance Balance	How effectively a system uses power to perform tasks	More output with less power
High-Performance Computing	Intensive Power Use	Systems that require large amounts of power for complex tasks	AI training clusters
Idle Power	Standby Usage	Power consumed when systems are not actively processing	Servers waiting for requests
Peak Power	Maximum Usage	Highest level of power used during heavy workloads	Training large AI models
Thermal Output	Heat Generation	Heat produced as a result of power usage	Cooling systems in data centers
Cooling Systems	Temperature Control	Systems used to manage heat from high power usage	Air or liquid cooling
Power Supply	Energy Source	Provides electricity to AI systems	Electrical grid, batteries
Edge Power Usage	Local Energy Use	Power consumption on smaller devices	Smartphones, IoT devices
Data Center Power	Large-Scale Usage	Power required for large AI operations	Server farms running AI models
Sustainable Energy	Efficiency Goal	Use of renewable energy to reduce environmental impact	Solar-powered data centers

The Watts Family highlights that intelligence comes with a cost—every AI system requires power, and understanding that power is essential for building efficient and sustainable technologies.

Watts Family (AI Power Usage Scale)

Definition

The **Watts Family** represents the real-time power usage of artificial intelligence systems, measured in watts (W). It shows how much power AI systems consume at a given moment as they process data and perform computations.

Watts Scale

1 Watt
10 Watts
100 Watts
500 Watts
1,000 Watts (1 Kilowatt)
10,000 Watts (10 Kilowatts)

100,000 Watts (100 Kilowatts)
1,000,000 Watts (1 Megawatt)
10,000,000 Watts (10 Megawatts)
100,000,000+ Watts (100+ Megawatts)

Key Characteristics

Measured in real-world electrical power

Higher watt values indicate higher processing demand

Used to represent the scale of AI systems from small devices to large infrastructures

Closely connected to the Chip Family, Energy Family, and Infrastructure Family

Examples

Low watts → small devices and basic AI functions

Medium watts → computers and advanced applications

High watts → data centers and large AI systems

Summary

The **Watts Family** provides a numerical representation of how much power artificial intelligence systems use in real time, helping to illustrate the scale and intensity of AI operations.

🧠 Student Insight

Watts show how much power AI is using right now.

AI Energy Family Introduction

The AI Energy Family represents the total amount of energy consumed by artificial intelligence systems over time. While the Watts Family measures the rate at which power is used at any given moment, the Energy Family focuses on the accumulated energy required to perform tasks, run systems, and sustain operations.

In artificial intelligence, energy is used every time a model is trained, a system processes data, or a response is generated. Large-scale AI systems, especially those operating in data centers, can consume significant amounts of energy due to the continuous processing of massive datasets and complex computations.

Energy is typically measured over time using units such as kilowatt-hours (kWh), which reflect how much power has been used during a specific period. For example, running a high-performance AI system for several hours or days results in a total energy cost that goes beyond the moment-to-moment power usage measured in watts.

The AI Energy Family works closely with the Watts Family, which provides the rate of power consumption, and the Chip Family, which determines how efficiently computations are performed. It also connects to the Infrastructure Family, where large-scale systems operate continuously and require long-term energy management.

Understanding the AI Energy Family helps students recognize that artificial intelligence has real-world resource implications. It is not only about performance and speed, but also about sustainability, efficiency, and responsible use of technology.

In simple terms, if watts measure how fast energy is used, energy measures how much is used over time.

AI Energy Family Breakdown Chart

Component	Role	Description	Example
Energy	Total Consumption	The total amount of power used over a period of time	Running an AI system for hours or days
Kilowatt-hour (kWh)	Energy Measurement	Unit used to measure energy consumption over time	1 kWh = using 1,000 watts for 1 hour
Energy Usage	Consumption Tracking	Total energy required for AI operations	Training a large model
Training Energy	Learning Cost	Energy used during model training processes	Weeks of GPU usage
Inference Energy	Response Cost	Energy used when AI generates outputs	Answering a user prompt
Energy Efficiency	Optimization Goal	Reducing energy use while maintaining performance	Efficient AI models
Energy Scaling	Growth Impact	Increase in energy use as systems grow larger	Bigger models = more energy
Data Center Energy	Infrastructure Demand	Total energy used by large AI facilities	Server farms operating 24/7
Cooling Energy	Temperature Control	Energy required to cool systems and prevent overheating	Air conditioning in data centers
Renewable Energy	Sustainability Source	Use of clean energy to power AI systems	Solar, wind-powered data centers
Carbon Impact	Environmental Effect	Emissions associated with energy consumption	AI training carbon footprint

Component	Role	Description	Example
Energy Management	Resource Control	Strategies to monitor and reduce energy use	Efficient scheduling, hardware optimization

The AI Energy Family reminds us that artificial intelligence operates within the physical world, where every computation consumes energy and every system has an impact on resources and sustainability.

Energy Family (Total Power Consumption of Artificial Intelligence)

Definition

The **Energy Family** represents the total amount of electricity used by artificial intelligence systems over time. It is measured in watt-hours (Wh) or kilowatt-hours (kWh) and shows how much energy AI systems consume while running.

Energy Scale

1 Watt-hour (Wh)
10 Watt-hours (Wh)
100 Watt-hours (Wh)
500 Watt-hours (Wh)
1,000 Watt-hours (1 Kilowatt-hour, kWh)
10,000 Watt-hours (10 kWh)
100,000 Watt-hours (100 kWh)
1,000,000 Watt-hours (1 Megawatt-hour, MWh)
10,000,000 Watt-hours (10 MWh)
100,000,000+ Watt-hours (100+ MWh)

Key Characteristics

Measured over time (not instant like watts)

Represents total electricity consumption

Increases the longer AI systems run

Directly related to cost and energy usage

Closely connected to Watts Family, Chip Family, and Infrastructure Family

Examples

Low energy → short AI tasks or small devices

Medium energy → daily AI usage on computers

High energy → training AI models and running data centers

Summary

The **Energy Family** provides a numerical representation of the total electricity consumed by artificial intelligence systems over time, helping to illustrate the overall cost and impact of AI operations.

🧠 Student Insight

Energy shows how much total power AI has used over time.

AI Infrastructure Family Introduction

The AI Infrastructure Family represents the large-scale systems and environments that support, power, and connect artificial intelligence technologies. While individual components such as chips, data, and models explain how AI works, infrastructure explains where and how these systems operate in the real world.

AI infrastructure includes data centers, cloud platforms, networking systems, and storage environments that allow artificial intelligence to function at scale. These systems provide the computing power, data access, and connectivity needed to train models, process information, and deliver results to users around the world.

Modern AI systems rely heavily on cloud-based infrastructure, where thousands of machines work together to handle massive workloads. This allows AI to scale efficiently, making it possible to process large datasets, run complex models, and serve millions of users simultaneously. Infrastructure also ensures reliability, security, and continuous availability of AI services.

The AI Infrastructure Family works closely with the Chip Family, which provides the hardware, the Watts and Energy Families, which manage power consumption, and the Data Family, which supplies the information being processed. It also supports the AI Architecture Family by providing the environment where all system components are deployed and connected.

Understanding the AI Infrastructure Family helps students recognize that artificial intelligence is not contained within a single device. Instead, it operates across global systems that require coordination, resources, and engineering to function effectively.

In simple terms, if AI is the system and chips are the engines, infrastructure is the environment that allows everything to run at scale.

AI Infrastructure Family Breakdown Chart

Component	Role	Description	Example
AI Infrastructure	System Environment	The physical and digital systems that support AI operations	Global AI platforms
Data Center	Processing Hub	Facilities that house servers and computing equipment	Large server farms
Cloud Computing	Scalable Platform	Remote systems that provide computing resources over the internet	AWS, Azure, Google Cloud
Servers	Compute Units	Machines that process data and run AI models	Rack-mounted servers
Networking	Connectivity System	Systems that allow communication between machines	Internet, fiber networks
Storage Systems	Data Management	Systems that store large volumes of data	Databases, cloud storage
Distributed Computing	Workload Sharing	Splitting tasks across multiple machines for efficiency	Parallel processing across clusters
Edge Infrastructure	Local Processing	Running AI closer to the user or device	Smart devices, IoT systems
Load Balancing	Traffic Control	Distributes workloads to prevent overload	Managing user requests
Security Systems	Protection Layer	Safeguards data and systems from threats	Encryption, firewalls
Redundancy	Reliability System	Backup systems to ensure continuous operation	Failover servers
Scalability	Growth Capability	Ability to expand resources as demand increases	Adding more servers dynamically

The AI Infrastructure Family reveals that artificial intelligence operates on a global scale, relying on interconnected systems that provide the power, storage, and connectivity needed to support intelligent technologies.

The AI Ecosystem Family

The AI Ecosystem Family is a connected group of artificial intelligence technologies, systems, behaviors, and applications that work together to help machines perform intelligent tasks. This ecosystem includes core AI systems, AI agents, agentic AI, AI autonomy, autonomous AI workers, and generative AI. Each part plays a different role in how modern AI systems think, learn, create, make decisions, solve problems, and interact with the world.

At the center of the ecosystem is artificial intelligence itself — the broad field focused on building machines and software that can perform tasks that normally require human intelligence. AI agents act as the systems that carry out goals and actions. Agentic AI describes the ability of AI systems to plan, reason, adapt, and pursue objectives with limited human guidance. AI autonomy represents the level of independence an AI system has while making decisions and taking actions. AI autonomous workers apply these capabilities to perform real-world tasks like digital employees or assistants. Generative AI adds the ability to create new content such as text, images, music, video, code, and designs.

The AI Ecosystem Family demonstrates that modern artificial intelligence is no longer just one single technology. Instead, it is an interconnected environment of systems, tools, intelligence, automation, creativity, and human collaboration. As AI continues to evolve, these technologies are becoming increasingly integrated into education, business, healthcare, communication, cybersecurity, research, and everyday life.

Understanding the AI Ecosystem Family helps students, educators, and readers see how the different parts of AI connect together to shape the future of intelligent systems and the digital world.

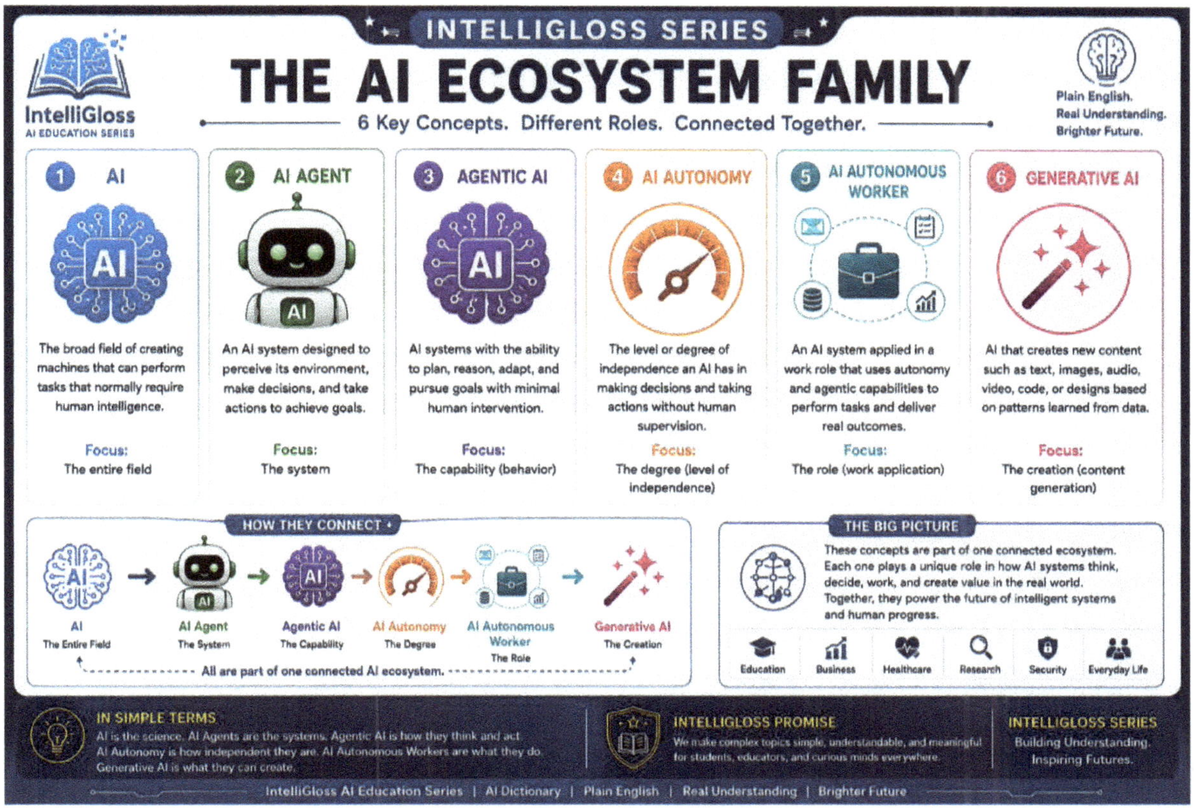

Ingredient Family Introduction

The Ingredient Family represents the essential components that come together to create an artificial intelligence system. Just as a recipe requires specific ingredients to produce a final dish, AI systems rely on a combination of foundational elements working together to function effectively.

Artificial intelligence is not built from a single component. It requires data to learn from, algorithms to guide processing, models to perform tasks, hardware to execute computations, and energy to power the entire system. Each of these elements plays a critical role, and the absence of any one component would prevent the system from operating properly.

The Ingredient Family provides a simplified way for students to understand AI as a system made up of interconnected parts. Instead of viewing AI as complex or mysterious, learners can begin to see it as something constructed from identifiable and understandable components.

This family connects directly with all other foundational families, including Data, Algorithm, Neural Network, Parameter, Chip, and Energy Families. It serves as an overview that brings these elements together into a unified perspective.

Understanding the Ingredient Family helps students recognize that artificial intelligence is built, not magical. It is the result of carefully combining the right components in the right way.

In simple terms, if AI is the final product, the Ingredient Family represents everything needed to build it.

Ingredient Family Breakdown Chart

Component	Role	Description	Example
Data	Learning Input	Provides the information AI uses to learn patterns	Text, images, audio
Algorithms	Instruction Set	Guides how data is processed and decisions are made	Sorting, classification
AI Models	Execution System	Performs tasks such as prediction or generation	Language models
Neural Networks	Processing Structure	Organizes how data is processed through layers	Deep learning models
Parameters	Learning Adjustments	Fine-tune how the model learns and makes predictions	Weights and biases
Tokens	Language Units	Breaks text into smaller pieces for processing	Words or subwords
Hardware (Chips)	Computation Engine	Executes calculations required by AI systems	GPUs, CPUs
Energy	Power Source	Supplies the energy needed to run systems	Electricity usage
Infrastructure	Support System	Provides the environment for AI to operate at scale	Cloud systems, data centers
Memory	Storage System	Stores and retrieves information for processing	Context memory
Knowledge	Understanding Layer	Represents meaning and relationships within data	Knowledge graphs

The Ingredient Family shows that artificial intelligence is built from a combination of essential components, each playing a vital role in creating intelligent systems.

The Frontend and Backend Family of Artificial Intelligence

How AI Systems Connect User Interaction to Intelligent Processing

Introduction

Every artificial intelligence system operates through two essential layers: the frontend and the backend. These layers work together to transform human interaction into intelligent responses, allowing AI systems to function smoothly and effectively.

The frontend is the part of the system that users see and interact with. It includes screens, input tools, and the display of results. Whether a user is typing a question, speaking a command, or uploading an image, all interaction begins at the frontend.

Behind the scenes, the backend serves as the processing engine of the system. It receives input from the frontend, manages data, connects to the AI model, and performs the computations needed to generate a response. The backend is where the intelligence of the system operates, using models, algorithms, and infrastructure to interpret and respond to user requests.

This visual illustrates how these two layers work together as a complete system. It shows the flow of information from user input to AI processing and back to the user as a result. By understanding this structure, students can see that AI is not a single tool, but a coordinated system of layers working together.

In simple terms, the frontend is where interaction happens, and the backend is where intelligence is created.

Every AI system has two sides: what you see and what actually does the thinking.

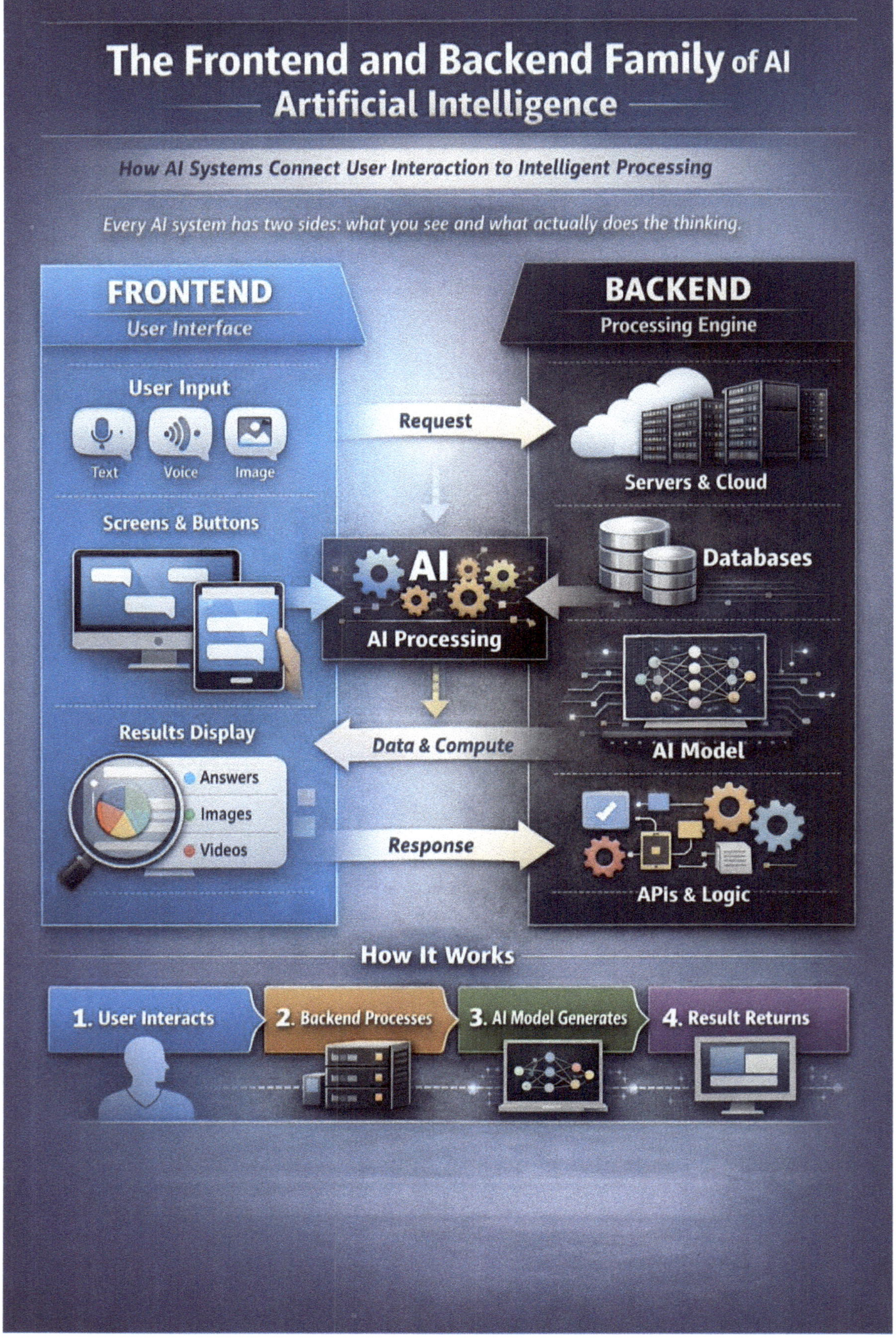
The Frontend and Backend Family of AI
Artificial Intelligence
How AI Systems Connect User Interaction to Intelligent Processing
Every AI system has two sides: what you see and what actually does the thinking.
FRONTEND
User Interface
User Input
Text
Voice
Image
Screens & Buttons
Results Display
Answers
Images
Videos
BACKEND
Processing Engine
Servers & Cloud
Databases
AI Model
APIs & Logic
Request
AI
AI Processing
Data & Compute
Response
How It Works
1. User Interacts
2. Backend Processes
3. AI Model Generates
4. Result Returns

AI Qubit Family Introduction

The AI Qubit Family represents the foundation of quantum computing as it relates to artificial intelligence. While traditional computing relies on bits, which can exist as either 0 or 1, quantum computing uses qubits, which can exist in multiple states simultaneously.

A qubit is the basic unit of quantum information. Unlike classical bits, qubits can take advantage of properties such as superposition and entanglement, allowing quantum systems to process complex computations more efficiently in certain scenarios. This opens new possibilities for solving problems that are difficult or impossible for traditional computers.

In the context of artificial intelligence, qubits have the potential to accelerate learning processes, optimize large-scale systems, and improve complex simulations. Although quantum AI is still in development, it represents a future direction where computational power can expand beyond current limitations.

The AI Qubit Family connects with the Chip Family, as quantum processors are specialized hardware, and with the Algorithm Family, where new types of quantum algorithms are designed. It also relates to the Parameter and Neural Network Families, as researchers explore quantum-enhanced learning models.

Understanding the AI Qubit Family helps students see that artificial intelligence is continuously evolving. It introduces the idea that the foundations of computing themselves can change, leading to new forms of intelligence and problem-solving.

In simple terms, if bits are the foundation of today's computing, qubits represent the foundation of tomorrow's possibilities.

AI Qubit Family Breakdown Chart

Component	Role	Description	Example
Qubit	Quantum Unit	Basic unit of quantum information	Quantum bit in a quantum computer
Superposition	Multi-State Ability	Ability to exist in multiple states at once	0 and 1 simultaneously
Entanglement	Connection Property	Linking qubits so they influence each other	Paired quantum states
Quantum Gate	Operation System	Performs operations on qubits	Quantum logic gates
Quantum Circuit	Processing Structure	Sequence of quantum operations	Quantum algorithms
Quantum Processor	Hardware Engine	Specialized chip for quantum computing	Quantum computer hardware

Component	Role	Description	Example
Quantum Algorithm	Computation Method	Algorithm designed for quantum systems	Optimization problems
Quantum Speedup	Performance Advantage	Faster processing for certain problems	Complex simulations
Quantum Noise	Stability Challenge	Errors caused by environmental interference	Qubit instability
Quantum Error Correction	Stability Solution	Techniques to reduce errors in quantum systems	Fault-tolerant computing

The AI Qubit Family introduces a new frontier in computing, where the limits of traditional systems are expanded, opening the door to more powerful and advanced forms of artificial intelligence.

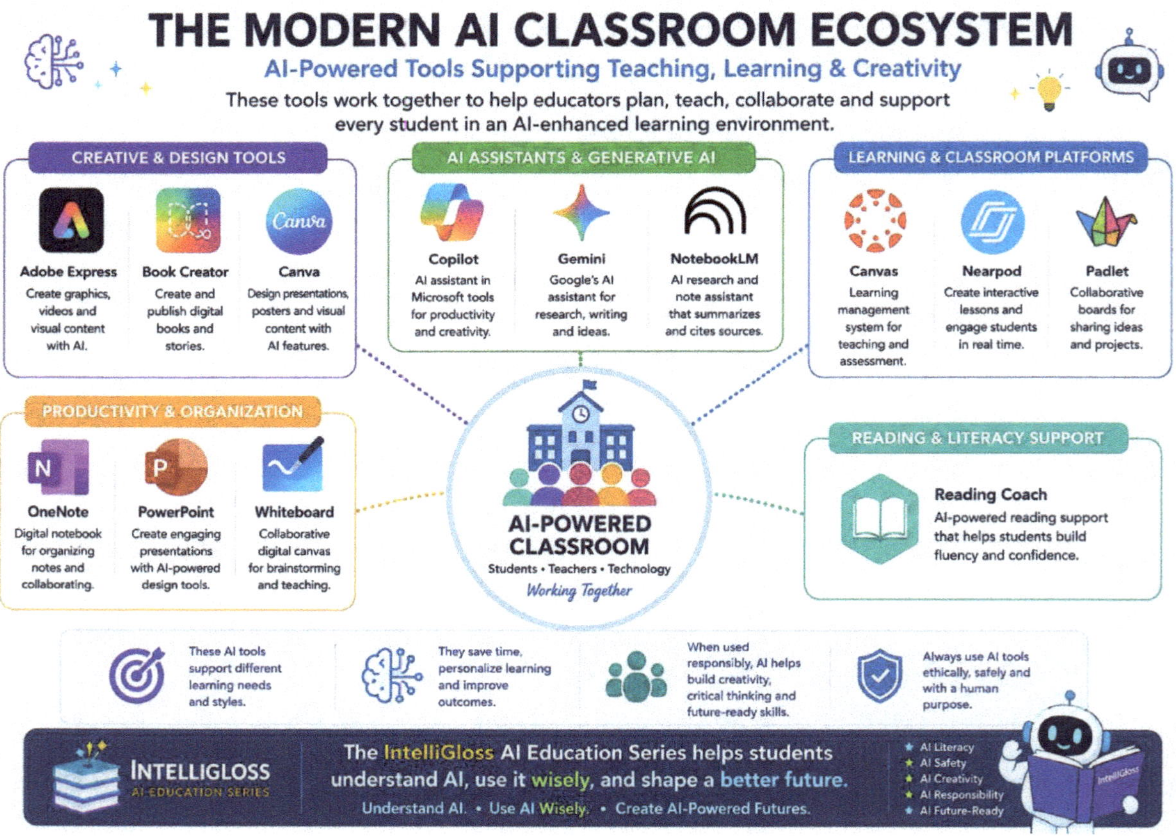

TABLE OF CONTENTS

INTRODUCTION PAGE

Level 1: Artificial Narrow Intelligence (ANI)

Understanding the AI Systems That Power Today's World

Why This Book Matters

Students today live in a world already shaped by ANI. Every time a voice assistant answers a question, a recommendation engine suggests a song, or a navigation app gives directions, **ANI is quietly working in the background**.

This book helps readers see these systems not as mysterious black boxes, but as understandable tools built by humans.
By studying how ANI operates, learners begin to see how logic, data, and creativity come together to form intelligent systems — and how humans can guide them responsibly.

For Students

Students will explore how narrow AI systems learn from patterns, make predictions, and help solve real-world problems.
They will understand that ANI is not science fiction — it is happening **now**, in healthcare, education, transportation, communication, and nearly every part of daily life.

By the end of this book, students will be able to:

- Identify what ANI is and how it differs from AGI and ASI.
- Recognize examples of ANI they encounter every day.
- Explain how data, algorithms, and human input shape intelligent behavior.
- Reflect on how AI changes society, jobs, and personal learning.

For Teachers

Teachers will find this book a **structured classroom guide** filled with rich discussion topics, vocabulary sections, and concept activities. Each chapter provides:

- **Teacher's Overview Page** explaining the main learning goals.
- **Classroom Discussion Questions** that promote critical thinking.
- **Real-World Case Studies** showing ANI in action.
- **Reflection Exercises** encouraging creative responses from students.

This textbook helps teachers introduce AI in a responsible, age-appropriate, and meaningful way — turning curiosity into understanding.

A New Kind of Literacy

Artificial Intelligence literacy is the next essential skill — just like reading, writing, and math once were.
To understand AI is to understand the new language of the world.
By mastering ANI, students learn to think critically about how machines make decisions, how data is used, and how humans remain at the center of every intelligent system.

This is not only a book about technology — it is a book about **human potential**.
When students learn how AI works, they also learn how **their own intelligence** works.

Chapter 1

The World of Artificial Narrow Intelligence

Introduction

Throughout human history, new forms of intelligence have reshaped the way societies function. The invention of written language allowed knowledge to travel across generations. The scientific revolution introduced new methods for understanding the natural world. The digital revolution placed enormous computational power into the hands of ordinary people. In the twenty-first century, humanity is experiencing another transformation—one driven by a new type of intelligence that exists not in the human mind but within machines.

This emerging form of intelligence is known as **artificial intelligence**, often abbreviated as AI. Artificial intelligence refers to computer systems that can perform tasks normally associated with human thinking, such as recognizing patterns, analyzing information, or making predictions. However, before exploring the more advanced concepts of Artificial General Intelligence (AGI) or Artificial Superintelligence (ASI), it is important to begin with the form of AI that already surrounds us today. This foundational stage is called **Artificial Narrow Intelligence**, or ANI.

Artificial Narrow Intelligence represents the first and most widely deployed level of machine intelligence. Unlike the human brain, which is capable of reasoning across many different subjects and situations, ANI systems are designed to focus on a specific task or a limited group of tasks. These systems are highly specialized. They do not possess awareness, imagination, or general understanding of the world. Instead, they perform carefully defined functions with remarkable speed and precision.

Even though ANI may sound technical or abstract, it is deeply woven into everyday life. Many of the technologies people rely on each day—from navigation systems and search engines to voice assistants and recommendation algorithms—are powered by Artificial Narrow Intelligence. Understanding ANI therefore provides an essential foundation for understanding how modern technology operates and how it will continue to evolve in the future.

Understanding Artificial Narrow Intelligence

Artificial Narrow Intelligence can be defined as a form of artificial intelligence that is designed to perform one specific task, or a small group of related tasks, within a clearly defined environment. These systems operate within strict boundaries. They learn patterns from data and use those patterns to make predictions or decisions, but only within the area they were trained to handle.

The key idea behind ANI is specialization. Just as a medical specialist focuses on a particular area of the body, an ANI system focuses on a particular type of problem. A program trained to recognize spoken language can convert speech into text with impressive accuracy, yet that same program cannot compose music, drive a car, or diagnose a disease. Each ANI system is built for its own purpose.

This specialization is not a weakness. In fact, it is what makes Artificial Narrow Intelligence so effective. By concentrating on a single problem, the system can process enormous amounts of information related to that problem and identify patterns that would be extremely difficult for humans to detect. As a result, ANI often performs certain tasks faster and more consistently than people.

However, it is important to remember that ANI does not truly "understand" the world in the way humans do. It does not possess awareness, feelings, or independent curiosity. Instead, it operates by analyzing patterns in data and applying mathematical models to produce useful results. The intelligence displayed by ANI systems is therefore practical and focused rather than general or philosophical.

The Mechanisms Behind ANI

To understand how Artificial Narrow Intelligence operates, it is helpful to examine the fundamental components that allow these systems to function. Most ANI systems rely on three core elements that work together to produce intelligent behavior: information, computational procedures, and iterative improvement.

The first element is **data**, which serves as the learning material for the system. Data can take many forms, including images, written language, numerical measurements, audio recordings, or sensor readings from physical devices. By examining large collections of data, an AI system can discover patterns and relationships that allow it to make predictions or classifications. For example, a system trained on thousands of labeled photographs of animals can learn to distinguish between different species by identifying visual patterns within the images.

The second element is the **algorithm**, which acts as the reasoning process of the machine. Algorithms are mathematical procedures that determine how the computer analyzes the data it receives. These procedures guide the system in identifying patterns, calculating probabilities, and determining which outcomes are most likely. In modern AI systems, many of these algorithms are based on machine learning techniques that allow the system to improve its performance over time.

The third element is **feedback**, which enables the system to refine its behavior. When an AI system produces an incorrect result, adjustments can be made to the underlying algorithm so that future predictions become more accurate. This process is often repeated thousands or even millions of times, allowing the system to gradually improve its performance. Over time, this cycle of data analysis, algorithmic processing, and feedback-driven correction produces systems that can perform their tasks with remarkable reliability.

Although this learning process may appear similar to human learning, it operates in a fundamentally different way. Humans rely on reasoning, experience, and emotional understanding, while ANI systems rely on statistical patterns and computational optimization.

ANI in Everyday Life

Artificial Narrow Intelligence is often described as an emerging technology, yet many people interact with it dozens of times each day without realizing it. The modern digital environment is filled with systems that quietly rely on ANI to provide faster services, more accurate recommendations, and improved decision-making.

In education, AI-powered learning platforms can analyze a student's responses and adjust lessons accordingly. If a learner struggles with a particular concept, the system may provide additional practice exercises or explanations. By personalizing instruction in this way, ANI systems help teachers support students with different learning styles and abilities.

In healthcare, machine learning models analyze medical images such as X-rays or MRI scans to assist doctors in detecting diseases at earlier stages. These systems do not replace physicians but instead act as analytical tools that can highlight patterns in medical data that might otherwise be overlooked.

Transportation systems also rely heavily on Artificial Narrow Intelligence. Navigation applications continuously analyze traffic patterns, road conditions, and travel times in order to recommend the fastest routes. Advanced driver-assistance technologies in modern vehicles use sensors and AI algorithms to detect obstacles, maintain safe distances, and assist with parking.

Communication technologies provide another example. Speech recognition systems convert spoken language into digital text, enabling voice assistants to respond to questions or perform tasks such as sending messages or setting reminders. Language translation tools use AI models trained on massive datasets of multilingual text to convert sentences from one language to another.

Even entertainment platforms rely on ANI. Streaming services analyze viewing patterns to recommend movies or television programs that match a user's interests. Video game characters often use AI algorithms to respond to player behavior, creating more immersive and dynamic experiences.

Across all of these examples, the pattern remains the same: each system performs a specialized function designed to improve efficiency, accuracy, or personalization.

Comparing Machine Intelligence and Human Intelligence

Although Artificial Narrow Intelligence can outperform humans in certain specialized tasks, it differs fundamentally from human intelligence. The human mind is capable of flexible thinking, creativity, emotional understanding, and moral reasoning. People can adapt to new situations, transfer knowledge from one field to another, and generate original ideas.

ANI systems, on the other hand, operate within strict limitations. They cannot apply their knowledge outside the domain for which they were trained. A program that excels at recognizing faces in photographs cannot suddenly begin writing essays or composing music unless it is redesigned and retrained for that new purpose.

Another key difference lies in awareness and intention. Humans possess consciousness and personal experience. They can reflect on their actions, question their assumptions, and consider ethical consequences. Artificial Narrow Intelligence lacks these qualities. It does not experience emotions, form beliefs, or pursue goals independently. Instead, it executes tasks according to instructions embedded in its algorithms.

These differences highlight an important principle: AI systems should be viewed as **tools that extend human capabilities rather than replacements for human intelligence**. By combining human creativity and judgment with machine precision and computational power, society can solve complex problems more effectively.

Teacher Overview

This chapter introduces students to the concept of Artificial Narrow Intelligence and establishes the foundation for the entire course. Students learn that AI is not a distant futuristic idea but a practical technology already embedded in modern life. Through discussion and examples, students begin to recognize how AI systems function and why they are described as "narrow."

Teachers may guide students toward identifying real-world technologies that rely on AI and encourage them to consider how these systems influence daily routines. Students should also begin to reflect on the differences between human thinking and machine-based decision-making. By exploring these questions, learners develop both technological awareness and critical thinking skills.

Reflection Activity

Students may be invited to reflect on their own interactions with AI technology. After learning about Artificial Narrow Intelligence, they can consider the ways AI appears in their daily routines. A short written reflection can describe how AI helps them study, communicate, travel, or entertain themselves. This activity encourages students to connect abstract technological concepts with their personal experiences.

Chapter 1 Review Materials

The World of Artificial Narrow Intelligence

Chapter Summary

Artificial Narrow Intelligence (ANI) represents the first and most widely used form of artificial intelligence in the modern world. Unlike human intelligence, which can think across many subjects and adapt to new situations, ANI systems are designed to perform specific tasks within a limited domain. These systems rely on data, algorithms, and feedback to identify patterns and improve their performance over time.

Throughout this chapter, students learned that ANI is already deeply integrated into daily life. Technologies such as navigation systems, voice assistants, recommendation engines, and automated medical analysis tools are examples of ANI in action. Although these systems can perform certain tasks faster and more accurately than humans, they do not possess creativity, emotional understanding, or independent reasoning.

The chapter also explored the key differences between machine intelligence and human intelligence. While machines rely on mathematical patterns and programmed instructions, humans use imagination, ethical judgment, and flexible thinking. This distinction highlights the role of AI as a tool designed to assist human decision-making rather than replace it.

Understanding Artificial Narrow Intelligence is an essential first step in learning about artificial intelligence as a whole. By recognizing how ANI operates, students begin to see how modern technology works and how future developments in AI may continue to shape society.

Reflection Section

Artificial intelligence is often described as a technology of the future, yet many AI systems are already part of everyday life. This chapter introduced the concept of Artificial Narrow Intelligence and demonstrated how machines can learn patterns from data to perform specialized tasks.

Students should take time to reflect on how AI technologies influence their daily routines. Consider the digital tools you interact with throughout the day. Many of these systems rely on AI algorithms that analyze information in order to provide recommendations, automate tasks, or improve efficiency.

Think about the relationship between human intelligence and machine intelligence. Humans possess creativity, emotions, and ethical judgment, while ANI systems focus on speed, accuracy, and data analysis. Understanding these differences helps us see how humans and machines can work together.

Reflect on the following questions and write thoughtful responses.

In what ways does Artificial Narrow Intelligence appear in your daily life?

Why do you think AI systems are described as “narrow” rather than general intelligence?

What are some advantages of using AI systems to analyze data or solve problems?

What abilities do humans have that machines still cannot replicate?

How do you think Artificial Intelligence will influence your future education or career?

Student Worksheet

Understanding Artificial Narrow Intelligence

Part A: Vocabulary Understanding

Write the correct definition for each term in your own words.

Artificial Intelligence

Artificial Narrow Intelligence

Algorithm

Data

Machine Learning

Part B: Concept Questions

Answer the following questions using complete sentences.

What is Artificial Narrow Intelligence?

Why are ANI systems considered specialized rather than general intelligence?

Explain how data helps AI systems learn.

Describe the role algorithms play in artificial intelligence.

Why is feedback important in improving AI systems?

Part C: Real-World AI Exploration

Think about technologies you use regularly.

List three technologies that likely use Artificial Narrow Intelligence. Then explain what specific task each system performs.

Technology 1:

Task performed by AI:

Technology 2:

Task performed by AI:

Technology 3:

Task performed by AI:

Part D: Critical Thinking

Imagine a world without Artificial Narrow Intelligence.

Write one paragraph describing how daily life might change if technologies such as voice assistants, recommendation systems, and navigation tools did not exist.

Chapter Quiz

Artificial Narrow Intelligence

Multiple Choice

Artificial Narrow Intelligence is best described as:

A. Intelligence that can perform all human tasks
B. Intelligence designed for a specific task or limited domain
C. A type of human learning system
D. A machine that has emotions

Which of the following is an example of Artificial Narrow Intelligence?

A. A human teacher explaining a lesson
B. A calculator solving a math equation

C. A recommendation system suggesting movies
D. A scientist performing research

What is the main role of data in an AI system?

A. To replace algorithms
B. To provide information that the system learns from
C. To eliminate the need for programming
D. To create emotions in machines

Algorithms in AI systems are best described as:

A. Mathematical instructions used to process data
B. Human decisions stored in computers
C. Hardware components inside machines
D. Electrical signals inside processors

Why is Artificial Narrow Intelligence called "narrow"?

A. Because it operates only on small computers
B. Because it performs specific tasks rather than general thinking
C. Because it uses limited electricity
D. Because it only works in laboratories

Short Answer

Explain the difference between human intelligence and Artificial Narrow Intelligence.

Give two examples of ANI used in everyday technology.

Why is Artificial Narrow Intelligence important for modern society?

Quiz Answer Key

Multiple Choice Answers

B – Intelligence designed for a specific task or limited domain

C – A recommendation system suggesting movies

B – To provide information that the system learns from

A – Mathematical instructions used to process data

B – Because it performs specific tasks rather than general thinking

Short Answer Sample Responses

Human intelligence can reason, feel emotions, and think across many subjects. Artificial Narrow Intelligence performs specific tasks using data and algorithms but does not possess awareness or creativity.

Examples may include voice assistants, navigation systems, recommendation engines, facial recognition systems, or automated medical analysis tools.

Artificial Narrow Intelligence improves efficiency, helps analyze large amounts of data, and supports many modern technologies used in healthcare, education, transportation, and communication.

Chapter 2

What Is Artificial Narrow Intelligence (ANI)?

Understanding the Meaning of Artificial Narrow Intelligence

Artificial Narrow Intelligence, commonly referred to as ANI, represents the earliest and most widely used stage of artificial intelligence development. It describes computer systems that are designed to perform a specific task or a closely related group of tasks within a clearly defined area. These systems are highly specialized. They do not possess the ability to think broadly across many different subjects in the way humans do. Instead, they concentrate their abilities on solving a particular type of problem with great accuracy and efficiency.

To understand ANI, it is helpful to compare it to human specialization. In the same way that a medical doctor may specialize in cardiology or neurology, an ANI system specializes in a particular function. A facial recognition program can analyze images and identify individuals based on facial patterns. A language translation system can convert text from one language into another. A navigation system can calculate the fastest route between two locations. Each of these systems performs its assigned task extremely well, but none of them can perform all tasks simultaneously.

This limited scope is the defining characteristic of Artificial Narrow Intelligence. While human intelligence is flexible and capable of shifting between many forms of thinking, ANI systems remain confined to the specific domain for which they were designed. Their intelligence is therefore described as "narrow," not because it is weak, but because it is focused on a particular objective.

Although ANI systems do not possess awareness, emotions, or creativity, they can perform complex tasks at speeds that far exceed human capability. This combination of specialization and efficiency has made Artificial Narrow Intelligence the foundation of modern digital technology.

The Origins of Narrow Intelligence

The development of Artificial Narrow Intelligence did not happen suddenly. It is the result of decades of research in computer science, mathematics, and cognitive science. Early computers in the mid-twentieth century were capable only of executing simple instructions. Programmers wrote precise commands that told the machine exactly what steps to follow in order to solve mathematical problems or perform calculations.

These early systems did not "learn." They simply followed fixed rules created by human programmers. However, researchers soon realized that many real-world problems could not be solved using rigid instructions alone. Tasks such as recognizing speech, interpreting images, or translating languages required a more flexible approach.

The breakthrough came with the development of machine learning, a field of artificial intelligence that allows computers to learn patterns from data rather than relying solely on explicit programming. Instead of being told every step to follow, a machine learning system studies large collections of examples and gradually improves its ability to make predictions.

As digital data became more abundant through the expansion of the internet and global communication networks, machine learning systems gained access to enormous datasets. Combined with advances in computing power and cloud infrastructure, these developments allowed AI researchers to create systems capable of performing highly specialized tasks with impressive accuracy. These systems became known as Artificial Narrow Intelligence.

Today, ANI powers many of the technologies that shape modern life, from online search engines to recommendation systems and automated customer service tools.

How Artificial Narrow Intelligence Learns

Artificial Narrow Intelligence learns by identifying patterns within large sets of information. This process is often referred to as pattern recognition. When an AI system is trained, it is provided with many examples that allow it to discover relationships between different pieces of data.

Consider the example of an image recognition system designed to identify animals in photographs. During training, the system analyzes thousands of images labeled with the correct category, such as cats, dogs, or birds. By examining these examples repeatedly, the system begins to recognize visual patterns that distinguish one category from another.

Over time, the AI model learns which features are most important for classification. For instance, it may detect that cats often have pointed ears, particular facial proportions, and certain fur textures. When the system encounters a new image, it compares these visual features with the patterns it learned during training. If the features match the learned pattern closely enough, the system identifies the image as a cat.

This learning process becomes more accurate as the system receives additional data and feedback. When the system makes mistakes, adjustments are made to its internal parameters so that future predictions improve. Through repeated cycles of training and correction, ANI systems become increasingly effective at performing their specialized tasks.

However, this learning remains limited to the specific type of data used during training. A system trained to recognize animals will not automatically understand how to recognize vehicles or buildings unless it is trained again with new datasets. This limitation reinforces the idea that ANI operates within narrow boundaries.

How Artificial Narrow Intelligence Processes Information

Although people often describe AI systems as "thinking," the processes that occur inside these systems are fundamentally different from human thought. Human thinking involves emotions, experiences, intuition, and conscious reflection. Artificial Narrow Intelligence, by contrast, operates through mathematical calculations and statistical predictions.

When an AI model receives input, such as a spoken sentence or a photograph, it converts that input into numerical representations that computers can process. Complex algorithms then analyze these numbers to determine patterns or probabilities. The system predicts which outcome is most likely based on the patterns it learned during training.

For example, a language translation system receives a sentence written in one language and predicts the sequence of words that best represents the same meaning in another language. The system does not truly understand the meaning of the sentence in a human sense. Instead, it relies on patterns found in massive collections of bilingual text.

This probabilistic approach allows AI systems to generate remarkably accurate results in many contexts. However, it also highlights an important limitation: ANI systems simulate understanding through mathematical models rather than genuine comprehension.

The Strengths and Limitations of Artificial Narrow Intelligence

Artificial Narrow Intelligence excels at tasks that require analyzing large quantities of data quickly and consistently. In many industries, AI systems are capable of detecting patterns that humans might overlook due to the sheer scale of the information involved.

In medical research, for example, AI systems can examine thousands of medical images to identify early signs of disease. In financial systems, machine learning models analyze transaction data to detect unusual patterns that may indicate fraud. In transportation, intelligent navigation systems continuously process traffic data to recommend optimal routes for drivers.

These capabilities demonstrate the extraordinary efficiency of ANI. Machines do not experience fatigue, distraction, or emotional bias. They can analyze massive datasets with remarkable speed and reliability.

Despite these strengths, Artificial Narrow Intelligence remains limited in several important ways. ANI systems cannot understand context beyond the data they were trained on. They cannot form independent goals or make ethical decisions. They lack creativity, emotional awareness, and the ability to reason across multiple domains.

These limitations mean that AI systems must remain under human supervision. Humans provide the goals, values, and ethical guidance that machines cannot generate on their own.

The Partnership Between Humans and Machines

The relationship between humans and Artificial Narrow Intelligence is best understood as a partnership. Humans design the algorithms, collect the data, and determine how AI systems should be used. In return, ANI systems assist humans by performing complex calculations, analyzing data, and automating repetitive tasks.

This partnership allows people to focus on activities that require creativity, empathy, and strategic thinking while machines handle tasks that demand precision and speed. In classrooms, AI-powered learning tools help teachers identify student strengths and weaknesses. In healthcare settings, AI assists doctors by highlighting patterns in medical records and imaging data. In agriculture, intelligent systems analyze environmental conditions to support more efficient crop management.

By combining human insight with machine analysis, societies can solve complex challenges more effectively than either humans or machines could accomplish alone.

Understanding this partnership is essential for the next generation of students. As AI technologies continue to evolve, future professionals will need to know not only how these systems operate but also how to guide them responsibly.

Looking Toward the Future

Artificial Narrow Intelligence represents the starting point of a much larger technological journey. Researchers and engineers are currently exploring the possibility of creating Artificial General Intelligence, a form of machine intelligence capable of reasoning across multiple domains in a way that more closely resembles human thinking.

Before such systems can exist, however, scientists must first understand how narrow intelligence functions. Every advancement in artificial intelligence builds upon the knowledge gained from developing ANI systems. The algorithms, data processing techniques, and learning models used in ANI provide the foundation for future innovations.

By studying Artificial Narrow Intelligence, students gain insight into how intelligent systems operate and how they influence modern society. This knowledge prepares them to participate in shaping the future of technology and to ensure that artificial intelligence continues to serve human needs and values.

The concept of "narrow" intelligence should therefore not be viewed as a limitation. Instead, it represents a powerful form of specialization that allows machines to perform certain tasks with extraordinary effectiveness. Within this focused capability lies the beginning of a broader transformation in how humans and machines learn, collaborate, and innovate together.

Chapter 2 Review Materials

What Is Artificial Narrow Intelligence (ANI)?

Chapter Summary

Artificial Narrow Intelligence, commonly known as ANI, is the most widely used form of artificial intelligence in the modern world. Unlike human intelligence, which can reason across many different subjects and situations, ANI is designed to perform a specific task or a limited group of related tasks. Its intelligence is focused within a clearly defined area, which is why it is described as "narrow."

Throughout this chapter, students learned that ANI systems rely on data and algorithms to perform their functions. Instead of understanding the world through emotions or experiences, machines analyze large amounts of information and identify patterns within that data. Through this process, AI systems are able to classify images, translate languages, recommend products, and assist with many other specialized activities.

The development of ANI has evolved over many decades. Early computers followed strict instructions written by programmers. As technology advanced and large datasets became available, researchers developed machine learning techniques that allow computers to improve their performance by learning patterns from data rather than simply executing fixed commands.

Although Artificial Narrow Intelligence can perform certain tasks with extraordinary speed and accuracy, it does not possess awareness, creativity, or emotional understanding. Its abilities remain limited to the tasks for which it was designed and trained. For this reason, ANI should be understood as a powerful tool that supports human decision-making rather than replacing human intelligence.

Understanding Artificial Narrow Intelligence provides an essential foundation for studying the broader field of artificial intelligence. By learning how ANI systems function, students gain insight into how modern technologies operate and how future AI developments may shape society.

Reflection Section

Artificial Narrow Intelligence plays an important role in modern life, even though many people interact with it without realizing it. From navigation apps and recommendation systems to speech recognition and medical analysis tools, ANI systems help people make decisions, solve problems, and access information more efficiently.

As technology continues to evolve, it becomes increasingly important for students to understand both the benefits and the limitations of AI systems. While machines can process vast amounts of data quickly, they do not possess human qualities such as empathy, creativity, or moral judgment. This means that human guidance remains essential in the design and use of artificial intelligence.

Reflecting on how ANI works can help students develop a clearer understanding of the relationship between humans and machines. Instead of viewing AI as something mysterious or futuristic, students can recognize it as a tool created by humans to extend their abilities and improve problem-solving.

Consider the following questions as you reflect on this chapter.

Why is Artificial Narrow Intelligence described as "narrow" intelligence?

How does ANI differ from human intelligence?

What are some advantages of using AI systems to analyze large amounts of data?

Why do AI systems rely heavily on data for learning?

In what ways do humans remain responsible for guiding and supervising AI systems?

Student Worksheet

Understanding Artificial Narrow Intelligence

Part A – Vocabulary Practice

Write a clear definition in your own words for each of the following terms.

Artificial Intelligence

Artificial Narrow Intelligence

Machine Learning

Algorithm

Data

Part B – Understanding the Concepts

Answer the following questions using complete sentences.

What is Artificial Narrow Intelligence?

Why are ANI systems considered specialized rather than general intelligence?

Explain how machine learning helped advance Artificial Narrow Intelligence.

Why do AI systems need large amounts of data?

How do algorithms help AI systems perform tasks?

Part C – Real-World AI Examples

Think about technologies that rely on Artificial Narrow Intelligence.

Identify three examples of ANI that you may encounter in daily life and explain what task each one performs.

Example 1:

Task performed:

Example 2:

Task performed:

Example 3:

Task performed:

Part D – Critical Thinking

Artificial Narrow Intelligence is powerful but limited. It can perform specific tasks very well but cannot think like humans.

Write one paragraph explaining why humans must remain responsible for guiding and supervising artificial intelligence systems.

Chapter Quiz

What Is Artificial Narrow Intelligence?

Multiple Choice

Artificial Narrow Intelligence refers to:

A. Intelligence that can perform all human tasks
B. Intelligence designed for a specific task or limited domain
C. A type of emotional intelligence
D. Human thinking enhanced by computers

Which of the following best describes ANI?

A. A machine that can reason across all subjects
B. A system designed to perform specialized tasks
C. A computer that experiences emotions
D. A robot that replaces human thinking

Machine learning allows computers to:

A. Develop emotions
B. Learn patterns from data
C. Eliminate the need for programming
D. Replace human decision-making completely

Algorithms are:

A. Mathematical instructions used to analyze data
B. Physical computer parts
C. Human decisions stored in machines
D. Electrical circuits inside processors

One major limitation of Artificial Narrow Intelligence is that it:

A. Requires electricity
B. Can only operate within the domain it was trained for
C. Cannot analyze data
D. Cannot follow instructions

Short Answer

Explain the difference between Artificial Narrow Intelligence and human intelligence.

Give two examples of Artificial Narrow Intelligence used in everyday life.

Why is Artificial Narrow Intelligence important for modern technology?

Quiz Answer Key

Multiple Choice Answers

B – Intelligence designed for a specific task or limited domain

B – A system designed to perform specialized tasks

B – Learn patterns from data

A – Mathematical instructions used to analyze data

B – Can only operate within the domain it was trained for

Short Answer Sample Responses

Artificial Narrow Intelligence performs specific tasks using data and algorithms, while human intelligence can reason, learn across many subjects, and understand emotions and context.

Examples may include voice assistants, recommendation systems, navigation apps, facial recognition software, or automated medical analysis tools.

Artificial Narrow Intelligence powers many modern technologies by analyzing large amounts of data, improving efficiency, and helping people make decisions in areas such as healthcare, transportation, communication, and education.

Chapter 3

How Artificial Narrow Intelligence Learns and Thinks

Level 1 – Preparing Students and Teachers for the Next Level of AI Understanding

Introduction

Learning is one of the most fundamental characteristics of intelligence. Human beings learn through experience, observation, reflection, and emotion. From early childhood, people gradually build knowledge by interacting with the world, remembering past experiences, and adjusting their behavior based on what they discover. Over time, these experiences accumulate and shape how individuals think, solve problems, and make decisions.

Artificial Narrow Intelligence, however, learns in a very different way. Machines do not possess curiosity, emotion, or personal experience. Instead, they learn by analyzing information and identifying patterns within large collections of data. Through mathematical models and computational processes, ANI systems can gradually improve their ability to recognize images, understand language, predict outcomes, or classify information.

Although machines do not learn in the human sense, their ability to process vast quantities of information allows them to develop specialized skills with remarkable accuracy. This chapter explores the mechanisms that allow Artificial Narrow Intelligence to transform raw data into useful predictions and decisions. By examining how machines learn, students and teachers gain a deeper understanding of how AI systems operate and why they have become such powerful tools in modern society.

Learning Through Data

The learning process for Artificial Narrow Intelligence begins with data. Data represents the information that the system studies in order to recognize patterns and relationships. Without data, an AI system has nothing to observe, measure, or analyze. For this reason, data is often described as the foundation of machine learning.

To understand the role of data in AI, it can be helpful to compare machine learning to the way humans learn through examples. A child who is learning to recognize animals may look at many pictures of dogs, cats, and birds. Over time, the child begins to notice patterns that distinguish one animal from another. These observations gradually form a mental model that allows the child to identify animals even in new situations.

Artificial Narrow Intelligence learns in a similar manner, but its observations are expressed through numbers rather than visual experiences. An AI system designed to recognize animals in photographs studies thousands or even millions of images labeled with the correct category. By examining these examples repeatedly, the system detects patterns in color, shape, texture, and spatial arrangement.

However, the machine does not perceive these images as humans do. Instead of seeing ears, tails, or fur, it analyzes the numerical values that represent each pixel in the image. Differences in brightness, color intensity, and geometric arrangement become mathematical signals that the system can measure. Through repeated exposure to these patterns, the system gradually develops the ability to classify new images correctly.

The quantity and quality of data play a critical role in the success of any AI system. The more diverse and accurate the training data, the better the system becomes at recognizing patterns in unfamiliar situations. In fields such as healthcare, transportation, and finance, massive datasets allow AI systems to detect subtle patterns that may be difficult for humans to notice.

The Role of Algorithms

While data provides the information necessary for learning, algorithms provide the method through which that learning occurs. An algorithm can be described as a structured set of mathematical instructions that guides a computer in analyzing data and producing a result. In artificial intelligence systems, algorithms determine how patterns are detected and how predictions are generated.

Algorithms serve as the reasoning framework of an AI system. They organize incoming data, evaluate relationships between variables, and calculate probabilities that lead to specific outcomes. Without algorithms, data would remain a collection of disconnected facts rather than a source of meaningful insights.

Different types of algorithms are designed for different types of problems. Some algorithms are used to classify information into categories, while others are designed to predict future outcomes based on past data. For example, recommendation systems used by streaming platforms rely on algorithms that compare a user's viewing history with patterns observed among millions of other users. By identifying similarities in preferences, the system predicts which movies or television programs a viewer might enjoy.

Although algorithms may appear intelligent, they do not possess awareness or understanding. They simply follow mathematical procedures that have been designed and refined by human engineers. These procedures allow machines to simulate decision-making processes by calculating which outcomes are most likely according to the patterns present in the data.

Through this interaction between data and algorithms, Artificial Narrow Intelligence systems develop the ability to perform complex tasks that once required human judgment.

Feedback and the Cycle of Improvement

Learning in Artificial Narrow Intelligence does not occur in a single step. Instead, it takes place through an ongoing cycle of analysis and correction that gradually improves the system's accuracy. This process is known as training.

When an AI system makes a prediction, the result is compared to the correct answer. If the prediction is incorrect, the system adjusts its internal calculations in order to reduce the error in future attempts. These adjustments are performed automatically by optimization algorithms that modify the system's internal parameters.

This feedback-driven learning process can be compared to the way students improve their understanding through practice and evaluation. When a student receives feedback on an assignment or exam, they gain insight into their mistakes and can refine their knowledge. Over time, repeated practice leads to greater accuracy and confidence.

In AI systems, this cycle of prediction and correction occurs thousands or even millions of times during training. Each adjustment brings the model slightly closer to the desired outcome. As a result, the system gradually becomes more reliable in its predictions.

Speech recognition systems provide a clear example of this process. When a voice recognition program encounters unfamiliar accents or pronunciation patterns, corrections provided during training allow the system to refine its understanding of spoken language. Over time, this repeated feedback enables the program to interpret speech more accurately across different voices and dialects.

This continuous improvement process allows Artificial Narrow Intelligence to adapt and refine its performance within the boundaries of its specific task.

How Artificial Narrow Intelligence Processes Information

The concept of machine "thinking" often leads to misunderstanding. Human thinking involves conscious awareness, reflection, and emotional context. Artificial Narrow Intelligence, however, processes information through computational analysis rather than genuine thought.

When an AI system receives input, such as spoken language or an image, that information is converted into numerical representations that computers can manipulate. Mathematical models then analyze these numbers to determine relationships and probabilities. The system selects the output that has the highest statistical likelihood according to the patterns learned during training.

For example, a language translation system processes a sentence by examining how words and phrases commonly appear together across large collections of multilingual text. Instead of understanding the meaning of each word, the system predicts which sequence of words in another language is most statistically consistent with the patterns it has observed.

This predictive method allows AI systems to produce remarkably accurate results even though they lack true comprehension. In essence, Artificial Narrow Intelligence simulates aspects of human reasoning through complex mathematical calculations.

Neural Networks and Digital Learning Structures

Many modern AI systems rely on computational structures known as neural networks. These systems are inspired by the organization of neurons in the human brain, although the resemblance is conceptual rather than biological.

A neural network consists of layers of interconnected units often called artificial neurons. Each unit performs a small mathematical calculation based on the information it receives from previous layers. As data passes through the network, these calculations gradually transform the input into a meaningful output.

For example, in an image recognition system, early layers of the neural network may detect simple features such as edges or color contrasts. Deeper layers combine these features to identify more complex structures such as shapes or textures. Eventually, the network produces a final classification, such as identifying whether an image contains a cat or a dog.

Neural networks allow Artificial Narrow Intelligence to handle highly complex tasks such as speech recognition, image analysis, and natural language processing. Despite their sophistication, these systems remain fundamentally mathematical structures that operate through numerical optimization rather than conscious reasoning.

The Limits of Machine Thinking

Despite the impressive capabilities of Artificial Narrow Intelligence, its form of thinking remains fundamentally limited. ANI systems cannot reason beyond the specific domain in which they were trained. They cannot imagine possibilities outside their training data or apply knowledge flexibly across unrelated tasks.

Human intelligence, by contrast, is highly adaptable. People can transfer knowledge from one area to another, develop creative ideas, and respond to unexpected situations with emotional understanding and ethical consideration. These qualities remain beyond the reach of current AI systems.

For instance, an AI system may recommend a song based on listening patterns, but it cannot experience the emotional impact of music. A medical AI may detect patterns in diagnostic images, but it cannot empathize with a patient receiving difficult news. These examples highlight the distinction between analytical capability and genuine understanding.

Recognizing these limitations is important because it reminds us that AI systems are tools designed to assist human decision-making rather than replace human intelligence.

Understanding Learning Through AI

Studying how Artificial Narrow Intelligence learns also offers valuable insight into human learning itself. The elements that define machine learning—data, algorithms, and feedback—reflect principles that appear in human education as well. Experience provides information, reasoning organizes that information, and feedback allows improvement over time.

In the classroom, these parallels can help students see that artificial intelligence is not mysterious or magical. Instead, it is a technological extension of logical reasoning and statistical analysis. By understanding how machines learn, students also gain a deeper appreciation for the learning processes that shape their own intellectual development.

Conclusion

Artificial Narrow Intelligence learns through a structured process that combines data analysis, algorithmic reasoning, and continuous feedback. This process allows machines to identify patterns, generate predictions, and perform specialized tasks with remarkable precision.

Although AI systems do not possess emotions, awareness, or creativity, their ability to analyze vast amounts of information makes them valuable tools in many fields. From healthcare diagnostics to speech recognition and transportation systems, ANI demonstrates how machine learning can enhance human capabilities.

Understanding how these systems learn and operate provides an essential foundation for studying more advanced forms of artificial intelligence. As researchers continue to explore the possibilities of Artificial General Intelligence, the principles developed through ANI remain the building blocks of future innovations.

In the end, the study of Artificial Narrow Intelligence reveals an important lesson: intelligence, whether human or artificial, begins with learning. By understanding how machines learn, students prepare themselves to participate in shaping the next generation of intelligent technologies.

Chapter Summary

Artificial Narrow Intelligence (ANI) learns in a structured and systematic way that is different from human learning. While humans learn through experience, emotion, and reflection, AI systems learn by analyzing data and identifying patterns within that data.

This chapter explained that data is the foundation of machine learning. AI systems study large collections of information to detect relationships and patterns. These patterns allow the system to classify information, recognize images, understand language, and make predictions.

Algorithms play a critical role in this process. They provide the step-by-step mathematical instructions that guide how data is analyzed and how predictions are generated. Without algorithms, data would not become useful knowledge.

Another important concept introduced in this chapter is feedback. AI systems improve through a cycle of prediction and correction. When mistakes occur, the system adjusts its internal parameters, gradually increasing accuracy over time. This process is known as training.

The chapter also explored how AI processes information using numerical representations and probability rather than true understanding. Neural networks were introduced as powerful structures that allow machines to process complex data such as images and language.

Finally, students learned that although ANI is powerful, it has clear limitations. It cannot think beyond its training, feel emotions, or apply knowledge across different domains. This reinforces the idea that AI is a tool designed to assist humans, not replace them.

Reflection Section

Artificial Narrow Intelligence learns in a way that is very different from human learning. While humans rely on experience, reasoning, and emotion, machines rely on data, algorithms, and feedback.

As you reflect on this chapter, think about how learning happens both in humans and in machines. Understanding these differences helps us better understand how AI systems work and how they can support human decision-making.

Consider the following questions and write thoughtful responses:

How does Artificial Narrow Intelligence learn differently from humans?

Why is data important in training AI systems?

How does feedback help AI systems improve over time?

What role do algorithms play in machine learning?

Why is it important to understand the limitations of AI systems?

In what ways can AI systems support human learning and decision-making?

Student Worksheet

How Artificial Narrow Intelligence Learns and Thinks

Part A – Vocabulary Practice

Write a clear definition in your own words for each term:

Data

Algorithm

Machine Learning

Feedback

Neural Network

Part B – Understanding the Concepts

Answer the following questions using complete sentences:

How does Artificial Narrow Intelligence learn from data?

Why are algorithms important in AI systems?

Explain how feedback improves AI performance.

What does it mean that AI uses "pattern recognition"?

How do neural networks help AI systems process complex information?

Part C – Real-World Application

Think about AI systems used in everyday life.

Identify three examples of AI and explain how each system learns or improves over time.

Example 1:
How it learns:

Example 2:
How it learns:

Example 3:
How it learns:

Part D – Critical Thinking

Artificial Narrow Intelligence relies on data, algorithms, and feedback to improve performance, but it does not truly understand information the way humans do.

Write one paragraph explaining why human thinking is still important even as AI systems become more advanced.

Chapter Quiz

How Artificial Narrow Intelligence Learns and Thinks

Multiple Choice

Artificial Narrow Intelligence learns primarily by:
A. Experiencing emotions
B. Analyzing data and identifying patterns
C. Making independent decisions
D. Thinking creatively

Data in AI systems is best described as:
A. Physical computer parts
B. Information used for learning
C. Electrical signals
D. Human instructions

Algorithms are:
A. Emotional responses in machines
B. Mathematical instructions used to process data
C. Hardware components
D. Random processes

Feedback in AI systems is used to:
A. Stop the system from learning
B. Improve accuracy through correction
C. Replace algorithms
D. Store data permanently

Neural networks are:
A. Human brain cells
B. Electrical circuits only
C. Layered computational systems that process data
D. Memory storage devices

One major limitation of Artificial Narrow Intelligence is that it:
A. Cannot process data
B. Cannot improve performance
C. Cannot think beyond its training domain
D. Cannot follow instructions

Short Answer

Explain how Artificial Narrow Intelligence learns from data.

What role do algorithms play in AI systems?

Why is feedback important in machine learning?

How do neural networks help AI systems perform complex tasks?

What is one limitation of Artificial Narrow Intelligence?

Quiz Answer Key

Multiple Choice Answers

B – Analyzing data and identifying patterns
B – Information used for learning
B – Mathematical instructions used to process data
B – Improve accuracy through correction
C – Layered computational systems that process data
C – Cannot think beyond its training domain

Short Answer Sample Responses

Artificial Narrow Intelligence learns by analyzing large amounts of data and identifying patterns within that data. These patterns allow the system to make predictions or classify information.

Algorithms provide the instructions that guide how data is processed and how predictions are made. They act as the reasoning framework of the AI system.

Feedback is important because it allows the system to learn from mistakes and improve accuracy over time through repeated adjustments.

Neural networks process complex data by using layers of interconnected units that transform input into meaningful output, such as identifying images or understanding language.

One limitation of Artificial Narrow Intelligence is that it can only operate within the domain it was trained for and cannot think or reason beyond that area.

CHAPTER 4: How ANI Differs from Human Intelligence

Introduction

To understand Artificial Narrow Intelligence, students and teachers must look beyond what machines *can* do and examine what they *cannot*.
At first glance, a computer that plays chess better than a world champion or an app that translates

speech instantly might appear "smart." Yet the kind of intelligence that lives inside machines is profoundly different from the living, emotional, and self-aware intelligence that defines human beings.
This chapter explores those differences — not to diminish AI's abilities, but to reveal the beauty and complexity of the human mind that inspires it.

Human Intelligence: Flexible, Emotional, and Reflective

Human intelligence is not a single skill; it is a vast landscape of thought, memory, emotion, and creativity.
When a person faces a problem, they draw upon imagination, past experiences, intuition, and moral judgment. They can connect unrelated ideas, create stories, dream of impossible inventions, and learn from failure.

A child, for example, can learn to ride a bicycle, write a poem, and comfort a friend — three very different acts requiring coordination, emotion, and empathy. The human brain is capable of adapting to entirely new situations without needing to be "reprogrammed." It learns through *experience*, guided by curiosity and purpose.

This flexibility gives humanity the ability to survive change. Whether inventing tools, forming societies, or solving global challenges, people think broadly, crossing disciplines and emotions with ease.

Artificial Narrow Intelligence: Focused and Functional

Artificial Narrow Intelligence is the opposite of this wide adaptability.
An ANI system is designed for *one specific function* and operates only within that domain. A chess-playing AI cannot prepare breakfast; a medical imaging system cannot compose music.
It possesses **computational power without comprehension**.

The strength of ANI lies in its precision. Given a task like detecting fraudulent credit-card transactions, it can analyze millions of data points in seconds — far faster than any person could. But if asked to explain *why* a transaction feels suspicious, it cannot provide reasoning in human terms. It identifies patterns and probabilities, not motives or emotions.

Where humans think **horizontally**, moving across ideas, ANI thinks **vertically**, diving deep into one narrow goal. Its world is made of numbers, not stories; of patterns, not feelings.

The Role of Emotion and Consciousness

Perhaps the greatest difference between humans and machines lies in emotion.
Emotions shape every human decision. Fear warns, joy motivates, empathy connects, and curiosity drives discovery. Emotions give meaning to knowledge — transforming information into wisdom.

ANI, by contrast, has no emotional experience. It can recognize a smile but cannot *feel* happiness. It can detect sadness in a voice but does not share the sorrow.
Without emotion, ANI cannot set moral priorities or make compassionate choices. It does not dream or regret; it does not imagine futures. Its existence is purely operational.

Consciousness — the awareness of one's own existence — also separates human and machine. Humans can reflect on their thoughts, question their beliefs, and change their behavior intentionally. ANI cannot question itself. It processes data mechanically, unaware that it is even processing.

Learning and Creativity

Humans learn through reasoning, mistakes, and imagination.
A student who draws a picture invents something new; a writer creates meaning from language. Creativity involves combining unrelated ideas in original ways — something ANI cannot truly do.

Although AI can generate art, music, or text that seems creative, it does so by recombining patterns from existing data. It does not *understand* beauty or purpose; it reproduces statistical possibilities based on what it has learned.
Human creativity, on the other hand, comes from desire, emotion, and a sense of meaning — qualities beyond code or computation.

Ethics and Moral Reasoning

Another defining difference is moral awareness.
Humans can distinguish right from wrong because they live within societies that value empathy, fairness, and responsibility. They can feel guilt, pride, or compassion — emotions that guide ethical behavior.

ANI does not understand morality. It follows instructions without moral context. A facial-recognition system, for example, cannot question whether it should be used; it simply functions as directed.
The responsibility for ethical use therefore rests entirely on human shoulders. This is why teachers, students, and developers must learn not only how AI works, but also how to use it wisely.

Memory and Context

Human memory is layered. We remember facts, but also emotions — the way an experience *felt*. These emotional memories shape how we react in the future.

ANI stores data but not meaning. It can recall information perfectly, yet it does not *understand* it. If the context changes, ANI must be retrained; humans simply adapt.
For example, a person who moves to a new city quickly learns new routes and customs through experience. A GPS navigation AI must be updated with new maps to function correctly.

This adaptability gives humans the edge in uncertain or novel environments — situations that ANI cannot easily navigate.

Language and Understanding

Language is a living symbol of human thought.
When humans speak, they do more than exchange words; they share emotions, culture, and intent. They read tone, humor, and hidden meaning.

ANI systems can process language through models that predict which word should come next, but they do not grasp *true meaning*. They simulate understanding by analyzing patterns in text, but they do not know the world behind the words.
For humans, language carries life. For machines, language is a sequence of data points — valuable but empty of feeling.

Interdependence — Humans and Machines Together

Although ANI and human intelligence are different, they complement one another.
Humans bring creativity, emotion, and ethics; machines bring speed, precision, and memory.
When combined wisely, this partnership enhances what both can do.
Teachers who use AI-based learning tools, doctors who rely on diagnostic algorithms, and scientists who analyze data with AI assistance all demonstrate this cooperation.

The goal is not to replace the human mind, but to **extend it** — to use ANI as a mirror that reflects our own intelligence and challenges us to grow wiser.

Conclusion

Artificial Narrow Intelligence and human intelligence belong to two distinct worlds — one mechanical, the other conscious.
ANI learns through data and algorithms; humans learn through experience and feeling. Machines process information; humans create meaning.
Understanding these differences allows students and teachers to appreciate both the promise and the limits of AI.

As humanity continues to design smarter systems, our challenge is to preserve the qualities that make us human — compassion, imagination, and moral vision.
In doing so, we ensure that technology remains our servant, not our substitute, and that Artificial Intelligence continues to reflect the best of human intelligence rather than replace it.

Chapter 4 Review Materials

How Artificial Narrow Intelligence Differs from Human Intelligence

Chapter Summary

This chapter explored the important differences between Artificial Narrow Intelligence and human intelligence. While AI systems may appear intelligent because they can perform complex tasks such as playing chess, translating languages, or analyzing medical data, their abilities are fundamentally different from the intelligence that humans possess.

Human intelligence is flexible and adaptive. People can learn across many subjects, combine ideas creatively, and adjust to unfamiliar situations. The human mind draws upon emotions, experiences, and intuition to make decisions. Humans also possess self-awareness and the ability to reflect on their own thoughts, which allows them to grow, learn from mistakes, and change their behavior intentionally.

Artificial Narrow Intelligence, by contrast, operates within a very specific domain. An ANI system is designed to perform one task or a limited set of tasks. It can process large amounts of information quickly and detect patterns within data, but it does not understand the meaning behind those patterns. Its intelligence is computational rather than emotional or reflective.

Another key difference between humans and machines lies in emotion and consciousness. Human decisions are shaped by feelings such as empathy, curiosity, and moral responsibility. These emotions allow people to develop ethical judgments and compassion toward others. ANI systems do not experience emotions or awareness. They follow algorithms and mathematical rules without understanding the social or moral implications of their actions.

The chapter also examined creativity and moral reasoning. Humans can invent new ideas, imagine possibilities, and interpret meaning in ways that machines cannot. Although AI systems may generate art, music, or text, they do so by analyzing patterns within existing data rather than by experiencing inspiration or purpose.

Finally, the chapter emphasized the partnership between humans and machines. Artificial Narrow Intelligence excels at analyzing large datasets and performing repetitive tasks with precision, while humans provide creativity, ethical guidance, and contextual understanding. By combining these strengths, societies can use AI technology to support human progress while preserving the unique qualities of human intelligence.

Reflection Section

Artificial Narrow Intelligence and human intelligence represent two very different forms of problem-solving. Machines are capable of processing vast amounts of information quickly, but they lack the emotional awareness and creativity that characterize human thinking. Understanding these differences helps students appreciate both the power of AI and the unique qualities of human intelligence.

Human intelligence allows people to adapt to unexpected situations, connect ideas from different areas of knowledge, and make decisions based on empathy and moral values. These abilities cannot be easily replicated by machines. Artificial Narrow Intelligence, on the other hand, excels in areas that require speed, precision, and pattern recognition.

Reflecting on these differences can help students understand the importance of responsible AI development. Technology should be designed to support human abilities rather than replace them. By recognizing the strengths and limitations of AI systems, students can begin to think about how future technologies should be guided by human values.

Consider the following questions as you reflect on this chapter.

What are the main differences between human intelligence and Artificial Narrow Intelligence?

Why are emotions important in human decision-making?

How does creativity distinguish human thinking from machine computation?

Why must humans remain responsible for the ethical use of AI technologies?

In what ways can humans and AI systems work together effectively?

Student Worksheet

Comparing Human Intelligence and Artificial Narrow Intelligence

Part A – Vocabulary Practice

Write a definition in your own words for the following terms.

Artificial Narrow Intelligence

Human Intelligence

Consciousness

Emotion

Creativity

Ethics

Part B – Understanding the Concepts

Answer the following questions using complete sentences.

Why is human intelligence considered flexible and adaptable?

How does Artificial Narrow Intelligence process information differently from humans?

Why are emotions important in human intelligence?

What role does creativity play in human problem-solving?

Why is ethical responsibility important when developing AI systems?

Part C – Comparison Activity

Complete the comparison below.

Human Intelligence Characteristics:

Artificial Narrow Intelligence Characteristics:

How They Can Work Together:

Part D – Critical Thinking

Imagine a future where AI systems are used in many areas of society, including healthcare, education, and transportation.

Write one paragraph explaining why it is important for humans to remain involved in decision-making when using AI technologies.

Chapter Quiz

How ANI Differs from Human Intelligence

Multiple Choice

Artificial Narrow Intelligence is best described as:

A. Intelligence that can perform many tasks like a human
B. Intelligence designed for a specific task or limited domain
C. A type of emotional intelligence
D. A form of human consciousness

One key difference between human intelligence and ANI is that humans:

A. Cannot process data
B. Possess emotions and self-awareness
C. Do not learn from experience
D. Cannot adapt to new situations

Artificial Narrow Intelligence primarily relies on:

A. Emotional judgment
B. Pattern recognition and algorithms
C. Human imagination
D. Moral reasoning

Why is creativity considered a uniquely human ability?

A. Because humans experience inspiration and imagination
B. Because machines cannot analyze data
C. Because AI cannot process information
D. Because creativity only exists in art

Why is ethical responsibility important when using AI systems?

A. Because machines make moral decisions on their own
B. Because AI systems require human guidance and oversight
C. Because AI replaces human intelligence completely
D. Because computers understand human emotions

Short Answer

Explain one major difference between human learning and machine learning.

Give one example of a task that ANI performs well.

Why is cooperation between humans and AI important?

Quiz Answer Key

Multiple Choice Answers

B – Intelligence designed for a specific task or limited domain

B – Possess emotions and self-awareness

B – Pattern recognition and algorithms

A – Humans experience inspiration and imagination

B – AI systems require human guidance and oversight

Short Answer Sample Responses

Human learning involves experience, emotions, and reasoning, while machine learning relies on data analysis and algorithms.

Examples may include facial recognition, speech recognition, recommendation systems, or medical image analysis.

Cooperation allows humans to provide creativity, ethics, and judgment while AI provides speed, accuracy, and data analysis.

CHAPTER 5: ANI in Education — How Smart Systems Transform Learning

Introduction

Education is one of the most powerful places where Artificial Narrow Intelligence (ANI) has begun to make a meaningful difference.
In classrooms around the world, intelligent systems are helping teachers manage lessons, personalize learning, and reach students in ways that were once impossible.
This chapter explores how ANI is transforming the way we teach and learn — not by replacing teachers, but by assisting them; not by controlling students, but by helping them discover their own potential.

ANI in education represents the meeting of human wisdom and machine precision — a partnership where data and empathy come together to support a more thoughtful, inclusive, and effective learning experience.

A New Partner in the Classroom

For most of history, education depended on one model: the teacher spoke, and students listened. While that model still plays an important role, today's classrooms are beginning to evolve. Artificial Narrow Intelligence systems act as silent assistants — analyzing student progress, identifying strengths and weaknesses, and adapting lessons to meet each learner's needs.

Imagine a teacher in a large classroom. Each student learns differently — some read fast, others need more examples, and some learn best through images. A human teacher can sense these differences but may not always have the time to respond to each one. Here, ANI becomes an ally. It collects information about student performance and helps the teacher adjust the pace and content for every individual.

This does not mean machines are teaching alone. It means that teaching has become a **collaboration** — where data helps guide compassion, and technology supports creativity.

Personalized Learning

One of the most remarkable achievements of ANI in education is personalization.
Traditional classrooms often move at one pace for all, but ANI makes it possible to customize learning for each student.

When a learner struggles with math concepts, an AI-based tutoring system can detect the difficulty and offer extra practice or simpler explanations.
When another student masters a topic quickly, the same system can provide advanced challenges to keep them engaged.

This approach transforms education from a one-size-fits-all model into a responsive, dynamic process.
It allows students to take charge of their learning journey while giving teachers insight into how each mind grows.

Teachers who once had to grade endless papers now receive automated feedback reports that show where their students excel and where they need help. With this information, teachers can spend more time mentoring and less time measuring — turning the classroom into a place of discovery rather than testing alone.

Breaking Barriers to Access

ANI also helps to break barriers that once limited education.
For students with disabilities, smart technologies can read text aloud, convert speech into writing, or translate information into sign language. For children in remote regions, online learning platforms powered by ANI bring high-quality education to their homes.

Language translation systems help students from different cultures learn together. A Tongan student, for example, can communicate with a classmate in Japan through real-time translation software. This creates a global classroom where understanding crosses borders.

Artificial intelligence, when used with care and ethics, makes learning more inclusive — ensuring that no student is left behind because of geography, language, or physical limitations.

The Teacher's Evolving Role

Teachers remain the heart of education. No machine can replace the warmth of human encouragement, the wisdom of experience, or the compassion of understanding.
ANI does not change the teacher's purpose; it **enhances** it.

With intelligent systems handling repetitive tasks like attendance tracking, grading, or data analysis, teachers gain more time to focus on what truly matters: guiding students, inspiring curiosity, and nurturing character.

Some teachers use ANI-powered dashboards to monitor student engagement in real time. Others use intelligent writing assistants to help students improve grammar and structure. In every case, the technology serves the teacher's mission — not the other way around.

As classrooms evolve, the best educators are those who learn to work *with* AI rather than against it, blending human empathy with digital precision.

Ethical and Emotional Balance

The integration of ANI in education also raises important ethical questions.
How much data should schools collect about students? Who owns that information? How can educators ensure that technology supports learning without reducing students to numbers or scores?

These questions remind us that intelligence alone is not enough — wisdom must guide its use. Teachers play a vital role in setting boundaries, protecting student privacy, and teaching responsible use of technology.

Emotional education is equally important. As students interact with machines more often, they must also learn to nurture the qualities that make them human — empathy, kindness, and moral judgment. AI can provide information, but only humans can provide meaning.

Learning Beyond the Classroom

ANI extends learning beyond school walls. Educational platforms powered by intelligent systems allow students to continue exploring subjects at home. They can ask questions, watch personalized lessons, and test their understanding instantly.

This kind of learning transforms education from a scheduled activity into a lifelong process. A student can study astronomy after dinner or practice a new language before bed, guided by a system that knows their pace and preferences.
For many students who once felt left behind, ANI opens doors to learning that were never available before.

Preparing Students for the Future

By using ANI today, students are also preparing for the world they will enter tomorrow — a world where intelligence is shared between humans and machines.

They will work in environments where data analysis, automation, and digital creativity are everyday skills.

Understanding how ANI functions helps students become more than users; it helps them become **creators** of technology. They learn to question how algorithms make decisions, how data shapes behavior, and how humans can design systems that serve the greater good.

Teachers, therefore, are not only teaching reading and math; they are nurturing digital citizens — thinkers who understand the power and responsibility of intelligent systems.

Conclusion

Artificial Narrow Intelligence has become a quiet revolution in education. It helps teachers reach more students, personalizes learning, and opens pathways to knowledge across cultures and abilities. Yet it also reminds us that the true essence of learning lies in human connection.

The partnership between ANI and educators shows a profound truth: when technology is guided by empathy, education becomes not just smarter but more human.

The future classroom is not a place where machines replace teachers, but a space where both work side by side — where logic and love, data and compassion, build a generation ready to lead with intelligence and heart.

Chapter 5 Review Materials

ANI in Education — How Smart Systems Transform Learning

Chapter Summary

This chapter explored how Artificial Narrow Intelligence is transforming education by supporting teachers and enhancing student learning. ANI systems are increasingly used in classrooms to analyze learning patterns, personalize instruction, and provide insights that help educators better understand student progress.

Artificial Narrow Intelligence functions as a supportive partner in the classroom rather than a replacement for teachers. Intelligent educational systems can analyze student performance, identify learning gaps, and provide tailored lessons that adapt to each student's pace and ability. By examining patterns in student responses, AI-powered platforms can suggest additional practice for difficult topics or offer advanced material for students who progress more quickly.

Personalized learning is one of the most important contributions of ANI to modern education. Traditional classroom instruction often moves at a single pace, which may not meet the needs of every student. ANI systems allow educational content to be adjusted based on individual performance, helping each learner progress in a way that matches their strengths and challenges.

Another important benefit of ANI in education is increased accessibility. AI-powered tools assist students with disabilities by converting speech to text, reading written material aloud, and providing visual or language support. Translation systems also enable students from different linguistic backgrounds to communicate and learn together, helping create more inclusive classrooms.

Despite these technological advances, teachers remain essential to the learning process. Artificial intelligence can assist with tasks such as grading, data analysis, and monitoring progress, but human educators provide guidance, encouragement, and emotional understanding that machines cannot replicate.

The chapter also discussed ethical considerations related to the use of AI in schools. Issues such as student privacy, data protection, and responsible technology use must be carefully managed to ensure that AI enhances education without compromising human values.

Ultimately, ANI in education demonstrates the powerful partnership between human intelligence and machine precision. When used responsibly, AI systems can help create learning environments that are more adaptive, inclusive, and supportive for students.

Reflection Section

The use of Artificial Narrow Intelligence in education represents an important shift in how students learn and how teachers support them. Instead of relying solely on traditional teaching methods, schools can now use intelligent systems to analyze learning patterns and provide individualized support.

While these technologies can improve efficiency and offer valuable insights, they also raise important questions about the role of technology in the classroom. Teachers must ensure that technology supports learning rather than replacing meaningful human interaction.

Students should also reflect on how these tools influence their learning experiences. AI-powered educational platforms can provide instant feedback, additional practice opportunities, and personalized lessons, but the responsibility for learning still belongs to the student.

Understanding how ANI operates in education helps students become thoughtful users of technology. It also prepares them to participate in a future where artificial intelligence will continue to shape how knowledge is created, shared, and applied.

Reflect on the following questions:

How does Artificial Narrow Intelligence help teachers support student learning?

Why is personalized learning important for student success?

How can AI technologies improve access to education for students around the world?

Why must teachers remain central to the learning process even when AI tools are used?

What ethical responsibilities should schools consider when using AI systems?

Student Worksheet

Understanding ANI in Education

Part A – Vocabulary Practice

Write a definition in your own words for the following terms.

Artificial Narrow Intelligence

Personalized Learning

Educational Technology

Accessibility in Education

Learning Analytics

Part B – Understanding the Concepts

Answer the following questions using complete sentences.

How does Artificial Narrow Intelligence assist teachers in the classroom?

What is personalized learning and why is it beneficial?

How can ANI help students who have different learning styles or abilities?

Why is it important to consider ethical issues when using AI in schools?

In what ways can AI systems improve educational access for students around the world?

Part C – Real-World Application

Think about technologies used in modern education.

List two examples of educational technologies that may use Artificial Narrow Intelligence and explain how they help students learn.

Technology 1:

How it supports learning:

Technology 2:

How it supports learning:

Part D – Critical Thinking

Artificial intelligence can analyze learning data and provide personalized support, but human teachers remain essential to the educational process.

Write one paragraph explaining why human teachers are still important in classrooms that use AI technologies.

Chapter Quiz

ANI in Education

Multiple Choice

Artificial Narrow Intelligence in education is primarily used to:

A. Replace teachers in classrooms
B. Assist teachers and personalize student learning
C. Eliminate school assignments
D. Replace all textbooks

Personalized learning means:

A. Every student receives the exact same lesson
B. Learning materials are adjusted to meet each student's needs
C. Teachers stop guiding students
D. Technology replaces teachers completely

Which of the following is an example of ANI in education?

A. A teacher explaining a lesson on the board
B. An AI-powered tutoring platform that adapts lessons to student performance
C. Students reading a printed textbook
D. A classroom discussion without technology

One benefit of AI in education is:

A. Reducing the need for teachers
B. Making learning more personalized and accessible
C. Removing all homework assignments
D. Eliminating classroom discussions

Why must ethical considerations be addressed when using AI in schools?

A. Because AI systems do not collect data
B. Because student privacy and responsible technology use must be protected
C. Because teachers cannot use computers
D. Because AI replaces school administrators

Short Answer

Explain how Artificial Narrow Intelligence can support teachers in the classroom.

Give one example of how AI technology can make education more accessible.

Why is the partnership between teachers and AI systems important?

Quiz Answer Key

Multiple Choice Answers

B – Assist teachers and personalize student learning

B – Learning materials are adjusted to meet each student's needs

B – An AI-powered tutoring platform that adapts lessons to student performance

B – Making learning more personalized and accessible

B – Because student privacy and responsible technology use must be protected

Short Answer Sample Responses

Artificial Narrow Intelligence can analyze student performance data, identify learning difficulties, and provide teachers with insights that help them adjust lessons to meet student needs.

AI tools can convert text to speech, translate languages, or provide online learning platforms that allow students in remote areas to access educational materials.

Teachers provide guidance, emotional support, and ethical understanding, while AI systems provide data analysis and personalized learning support.

CHAPTER 6: ANI in Healthcare — How Machines Help Save Lives

Introduction

Health is the foundation of human life, and caring for it has always been one of society's most noble responsibilities.
Today, Artificial Narrow Intelligence (ANI) stands beside doctors, nurses, and researchers as a quiet yet powerful ally.
While machines do not feel compassion, they can process information at speeds far beyond human capacity — finding early signs of disease, predicting treatment outcomes, and supporting medical professionals in making life-saving decisions.

This chapter explores how ANI has entered hospitals, clinics, and laboratories around the world, transforming medicine from reactive care into predictive, data-driven understanding.

A New Era of Healing

For centuries, medicine relied on the careful eyes and experience of physicians. Diagnosis depended on observation, memory, and instinct.
But the human eye can only see so much, and the human brain can only remember so many details. As medical data grew — millions of scans, test results, and patient histories — doctors faced an overwhelming challenge: how to analyze it all in time to help each patient.

Artificial Narrow Intelligence became the bridge between data and diagnosis.
By training on vast medical datasets, ANI systems learned to recognize patterns invisible to even the most skilled specialists.
In radiology, an AI can examine thousands of X-rays or MRIs and identify suspicious spots that might indicate tumors. In pathology, it can analyze cell images for irregularities too small for the human eye.

These systems do not replace doctors; they empower them — giving second opinions, highlighting potential errors, and offering evidence-based insights that speed up critical decisions.

Early Detection and Prevention

One of the greatest contributions of ANI to healthcare is **early detection**.
Diseases like cancer, diabetes, and heart conditions often progress silently before symptoms appear. ANI tools analyze subtle changes in medical images or patient data to flag risks before they become dangerous.

For instance, an algorithm trained on thousands of mammograms can learn what early-stage breast cancer looks like and alert doctors when similar patterns appear in a new patient.
In cardiology, smart wearables track heart rhythms in real time, warning users and physicians about irregular beats that might signal an impending heart event.

Early intervention saves lives. With ANI's ability to process and interpret continuous streams of data, prevention is becoming as important as treatment. Medicine is shifting from *reacting to illness* toward *protecting health before illness begins.*

Personalized Medicine

No two bodies are the same, and no disease behaves identically in every person. Traditional medicine often followed standardized treatment paths; however, ANI introduces a new vision called **personalized medicine**.

By comparing an individual's genetic makeup, lifestyle, and medical history with millions of other cases, ANI can help doctors design treatments tailored to each patient.
This precision ensures that the right medicine reaches the right person at the right time.

For example, in oncology, intelligent systems predict which chemotherapy drugs will be most effective based on the unique genetic profile of a tumor.
In pharmacology, AI helps design drugs faster by simulating how molecules will interact with cells before they ever reach a laboratory.

Through these innovations, medicine is moving closer to the dream of truly individualized care — healing that understands not just disease, but the person who carries it.

Robotics and Surgical Assistance

In modern hospitals, some of the most delicate operations are performed with the help of ANI-guided robots.
These surgical systems translate the movements of a surgeon's hands into precise micro-motions, allowing for minimally invasive procedures with smaller incisions and faster recovery times.

During surgery, ANI algorithms monitor vital signs, adjust instruments, and provide real-time feedback. The surgeon remains in control, but the machine enhances stability and accuracy.
This partnership between human skill and mechanical precision reduces error and pain while expanding the possibilities of what can be safely achieved in the operating room.

Public Health and Disease Prediction

Beyond individual patients, ANI also serves entire communities.
Health organizations use AI systems to predict the spread of infectious diseases by analyzing travel data, social media trends, and climate patterns.
During pandemics, such systems help identify high-risk zones and allocate medical resources efficiently.

For example, predictive models can estimate how a virus might spread across regions, allowing governments to act before hospitals become overwhelmed.
This level of foresight — powered by data and algorithms — transforms healthcare into a proactive force protecting both people and populations.

Ethical Responsibilities in Medical AI

With such power comes deep ethical responsibility.
Medical data contains the most personal information a human can share, and its protection must be absolute.
Students and future scientists must understand that every dataset represents real lives and private stories.

Hospitals and researchers follow strict privacy laws to ensure that patient identities remain anonymous. Still, ethical questions continue: Who owns medical data? How do we prevent bias in algorithms trained on limited populations?
If an AI misdiagnoses a case, who is accountable — the doctor, the developer, or the system itself?

These issues remind us that technology can only be as ethical as the people who design and use it. Compassion, transparency, and fairness must always guide innovation in healthcare.

Human Touch in a Digital Age

No matter how advanced technology becomes, the human touch remains irreplaceable.
A machine can detect illness, but it cannot comfort a frightened patient. It can recommend treatment, but it cannot hold a hand or offer hope.
Doctors, nurses, and caregivers embody empathy — something that no algorithm can replicate.

Artificial Narrow Intelligence strengthens medical practice, but humanity gives it purpose.
Together, they form a complete circle of care: data for accuracy, emotion for healing.

Conclusion

Artificial Narrow Intelligence is transforming healthcare from the inside out.
It assists in diagnosis, predicts disease, designs personalized treatment plans, and enhances surgeries. Yet behind every data point stands a doctor, a nurse, a researcher — a human guiding the system toward compassion and ethical care.

This partnership illustrates the essence of intelligence itself: machines bring speed and precision; humans bring wisdom and empathy.
As students and teachers study how ANI saves lives, they are also learning an even greater lesson — that technology's highest purpose is not to replace humanity, but to help it thrive.

Chapter 6 Review Materials

ANI in Healthcare — How Machines Help Save Lives

Chapter Summary

This chapter explored how Artificial Narrow Intelligence is transforming healthcare by assisting medical professionals in diagnosing diseases, predicting health risks, and improving treatment decisions. As medical information continues to grow rapidly, healthcare systems increasingly rely on intelligent technologies to analyze large amounts of data quickly and accurately.

Artificial Narrow Intelligence systems are capable of recognizing patterns in medical data such as X-rays, MRI scans, laboratory results, and patient records. These systems can identify signs of disease that might be difficult for humans to detect, helping doctors make faster and more accurate diagnoses. In many hospitals, AI tools act as supportive assistants that provide second opinions and highlight potential concerns for further investigation.

One of the most important contributions of ANI to healthcare is early detection. By analyzing subtle changes in medical data, AI systems can identify warning signs of conditions such as cancer, heart disease, or diabetes before symptoms become severe. Early detection allows doctors to begin treatment sooner, which can greatly improve patient outcomes.

Artificial Narrow Intelligence also supports the development of personalized medicine. By analyzing an individual's medical history, genetic information, and lifestyle factors, AI systems can help doctors design treatments tailored to each patient. This approach improves the effectiveness of medical care by ensuring that treatments are suited to the unique characteristics of each person.

In addition, ANI assists surgeons through advanced robotic systems that enhance precision during delicate operations. These systems help reduce surgical risks, minimize recovery time, and improve patient safety. Public health organizations also use AI models to analyze disease patterns and predict the spread of infectious illnesses, allowing governments and healthcare providers to respond more effectively during health emergencies.

Despite these technological advances, the chapter emphasizes that human compassion and ethical responsibility remain central to healthcare. While AI systems can process data and assist with diagnosis, only human caregivers can provide emotional support, empathy, and moral judgment. The collaboration between medical professionals and intelligent technologies demonstrates how human intelligence and machine precision can work together to improve health and save lives.

Reflection Section

Artificial Narrow Intelligence is changing the way healthcare professionals diagnose diseases, analyze medical data, and treat patients. Intelligent systems can detect patterns in medical images, analyze patient records, and predict potential health risks with remarkable speed and accuracy.

However, the use of AI in healthcare also raises important questions about ethics, responsibility, and patient privacy. Medical information is highly personal, and it must be handled with great care to protect patient dignity and trust. Healthcare providers must ensure that AI technologies are used responsibly and that human judgment remains central to all medical decisions.

Students should also consider the role that compassion plays in healthcare. While machines can assist with analysis and diagnosis, they cannot provide emotional support or understand the fears and hopes of patients. Human caregivers bring empathy and understanding to medical care, which remains essential to healing.

Reflect on the following questions:

How does Artificial Narrow Intelligence assist doctors and medical professionals?

Why is early detection important for treating diseases?

How does personalized medicine improve patient care?

Why must ethical responsibility guide the use of AI in healthcare?

Why will human caregivers always remain important in the medical field?

Student Worksheet

Understanding Artificial Narrow Intelligence in Healthcare

Part A – Vocabulary Practice

Write a definition in your own words for the following terms.

Artificial Narrow Intelligence

Medical Diagnosis

Personalized Medicine

Surgical Robotics

Public Health

Medical Ethics

Part B – Understanding the Concepts

Answer the following questions using complete sentences.

How does Artificial Narrow Intelligence help doctors analyze medical data?

Why is early detection of diseases important for improving health outcomes?

What is personalized medicine, and how does AI help make it possible?

How do robotic surgical systems assist doctors during operations?

Why is protecting patient data important when using AI in healthcare?

Part C – Real-World Application

Think about technologies used in healthcare.

Identify two examples of how Artificial Narrow Intelligence may be used in medical settings and explain how they help patients.

Example 1:

How it helps healthcare professionals:

Example 2:

How it helps healthcare professionals:

Part D – Critical Thinking

Artificial intelligence can analyze medical data and support doctors, but it cannot replace the compassion and ethical judgment of human caregivers.

Write one paragraph explaining why human empathy is still essential in healthcare even when advanced technology is used.

Chapter Quiz

ANI in Healthcare

Multiple Choice

Artificial Narrow Intelligence helps doctors primarily by:

A. Replacing medical professionals
B. Analyzing medical data and assisting with diagnosis
C. Eliminating the need for hospitals
D. Performing emotional counseling

One major benefit of AI in healthcare is:

A. Slowing down medical research
B. Early detection of diseases
C. Removing human doctors
D. Eliminating patient records

Personalized medicine means:

A. Every patient receives the same treatment
B. Treatments are designed based on individual patient data
C. Patients diagnose themselves
D. AI replaces doctors completely

Surgical robots help doctors by:

A. Performing surgeries completely alone
B. Enhancing precision and assisting surgeons during procedures
C. Eliminating the need for training
D. Replacing operating rooms

Ethical concerns in medical AI often focus on:

A. Electricity use in hospitals
B. Protecting patient privacy and preventing bias in data
C. Removing doctors from decision-making
D. Increasing hospital costs

Short Answer

Explain one way Artificial Narrow Intelligence helps detect diseases.

Give one example of how AI technology assists doctors during treatment.

Why is the partnership between AI systems and human caregivers important in healthcare?

Quiz Answer Key

Multiple Choice Answers

B – Analyzing medical data and assisting with diagnosis

B – Early detection of diseases

B – Treatments are designed based on individual patient data

B – Enhancing precision and assisting surgeons during procedures

B – Protecting patient privacy and preventing bias in data

Short Answer Sample Responses

AI systems analyze medical images or patient records to identify early signs of diseases such as cancer or heart conditions.

AI-assisted surgical robots help surgeons perform delicate operations with greater accuracy and stability.

AI systems provide speed and data analysis, while human caregivers provide empathy, judgment, and ethical decision-making.

CHAPTER 7 ANI in Transportation — How Machines Move the Modern World

Introduction

Transportation is the lifeline of civilization.
It connects families, delivers goods, and keeps entire economies in motion. Yet as cities grow and roads become crowded, the need for safer, faster, and more efficient movement has never been greater.
Here, Artificial Narrow Intelligence (ANI) plays a transformative role. From self-driving cars to smart traffic lights, intelligent systems are quietly steering the modern world toward a new era of mobility.

This chapter explains how ANI analyzes routes, predicts traffic, and assists drivers and pilots alike. It also explores the delicate balance between automation and human responsibility — a partnership that is redefining how humanity travels.

The Rise of Smart Mobility

For centuries, transportation advanced through mechanical innovation: the wheel, the steam engine, the automobile, the airplane.
Today, progress is guided not only by metal and fuel but also by data and algorithms.
ANI has entered every layer of transportation — controlling traffic signals in busy cities, optimizing airline routes across continents, and helping ships navigate turbulent seas.

A self-driving car, for example, is powered by thousands of narrow AI subsystems working together. Cameras detect objects, radar measures distance, and neural networks interpret the environment in real time. The car does not "see" as humans do; it calculates. Every frame of video becomes a matrix of numbers processed in milliseconds, allowing it to recognize pedestrians, read stop signs, and adjust speed automatically.

This shift marks the birth of **smart mobility**, where vehicles no longer depend solely on human reflexes but on shared intelligence distributed through sensors and networks.

Data — The Fuel of Intelligent Transportation

In the traditional world, engines ran on gasoline. In the world of ANI, they run on data.
Each sensor — a camera, GPS unit, or speed detector — generates a continuous stream of information. Artificial Narrow Intelligence systems process this data to detect hazards, predict congestion, and guide decision-making.

Consider city traffic. Every driver contributes unknowingly to a massive digital heartbeat of motion. ANI collects this information through navigation apps, satellites, and public sensors, transforming it into traffic maps that update in seconds.
When a road accident occurs, the system redirects vehicles, adjusts signal timings, and balances flow — reducing both delay and pollution.

Through data, transportation becomes more than movement; it becomes *communication* — vehicles, roads, and humans speaking a common digital language of efficiency.

Safety and Prediction

Safety has always been the highest goal of transportation.
Every year, millions of accidents happen due to fatigue, distraction, or poor judgment. ANI aims to reduce these risks by predicting danger before it strikes.

Driver-assistance systems now monitor lane positions, detect blind-spot vehicles, and apply brakes automatically when collisions are imminent.
Aircraft navigation systems use ANI to analyze weather conditions and turbulence patterns, guiding pilots toward smoother and safer routes.
Even rail networks employ predictive maintenance algorithms that listen to the vibrations of wheels and tracks, detecting microscopic fractures before they cause accidents.

Machines cannot feel fear or urgency, but they can calculate probability with astonishing precision — a new form of foresight that turns reaction into prevention.

Logistics and Global Movement

Beyond roads and skies lies a vast network of shipping routes and supply chains that power global trade.
Artificial Narrow Intelligence manages this invisible machinery of commerce with unmatched accuracy.

In shipping ports, AI systems schedule cranes, track containers, and optimize vessel loading times. In trucking, intelligent routing software determines the most efficient paths based on fuel prices, weather, and delivery deadlines.
Airlines rely on predictive models to plan flight schedules that minimize fuel consumption and carbon emissions.

The result is a world that moves not only faster but also smarter. Goods reach markets more reliably, reducing waste and cost — a vital achievement for an interconnected planet.

Public Transportation and Urban Planning

Cities are ecosystems of motion. Buses, subways, and trains must operate in harmony to keep millions of people moving each day.
ANI assists city planners by analyzing ridership data and predicting how populations travel over time.

Smart ticketing systems forecast demand, while intelligent scheduling tools coordinate departures to prevent overcrowding.
During emergencies, ANI systems reroute traffic, adjust service intervals, and communicate updates instantly to passengers.

By turning raw data into understanding, ANI gives cities the ability to breathe — adapting in real time to the rhythm of human life.

The Human Element

Even as automation expands, human oversight remains essential.
Pilots, drivers, engineers, and traffic controllers still make the final decisions because only humans can interpret context, emotion, and ethics.
A self-driving car may know how to avoid collisions, but it cannot understand moral choices — such as when to prioritize one life over another.

Therefore, transportation in the age of ANI is not about removing people; it is about **redefining their role**. Humans provide judgment and empathy; machines provide speed and precision. Together, they form a cooperative system where safety and intelligence coexist.

Environmental Benefits

ANI also plays a crucial role in protecting the planet.
By optimizing routes and reducing idle time, intelligent systems lower fuel consumption and carbon emissions.
Electric vehicles use AI to balance power loads and extend battery life, while smart traffic grids cut unnecessary congestion.

Every efficient journey saves energy, and every saved kilowatt represents a step toward a cleaner Earth. In this way, ANI does more than move vehicles — it helps sustain the future of mobility for generations to come.

Challenges and Ethical Concerns

The road to intelligent transportation is not without challenges.
Data privacy, system errors, and algorithmic bias remain serious concerns. A malfunctioning sensor or hacked system could cause catastrophic results.
Governments and engineers must therefore work together to create safety standards that evolve with technology.

Ethical debates also continue: Who is responsible when an autonomous vehicle makes a mistake? How should algorithms prioritize safety in unpredictable scenarios?
These questions remind us that technology is only as moral as its makers — and that education, transparency, and regulation must guide every innovation on the road.

Conclusion

Artificial Narrow Intelligence is reshaping transportation from the ground up.
It reads the flow of traffic, predicts danger, manages logistics, and connects continents with digital precision. Yet its greatest achievement lies in partnership — the union of machine accuracy and human awareness.

As students and teachers study ANI's role in mobility, they are witnessing more than a technological upgrade; they are observing a transformation in civilization's heartbeat.
From the wheel to the algorithm, every advance in transportation has carried humanity forward — and with ANI, the journey continues toward a world where movement is not just faster, but wiser and safer for all.

Chapter 7 Review Materials

ANI in Transportation — How Machines Move the Modern World

Chapter Summary

This chapter explored how Artificial Narrow Intelligence is transforming transportation systems around the world. As cities grow and transportation networks become more complex, intelligent technologies are helping improve safety, efficiency, and coordination across roads, air travel, shipping routes, and public transit systems.

Artificial Narrow Intelligence plays an important role in modern mobility by analyzing large amounts of transportation data. Systems powered by AI monitor traffic conditions, optimize routes, and assist drivers through advanced safety features. Navigation platforms analyze real-time information from satellites, sensors, and user reports to guide vehicles along the fastest and safest paths.

One of the most visible applications of ANI in transportation is the development of self-driving vehicles. These systems rely on multiple sensors such as cameras, radar, and GPS devices to observe their surroundings. Artificial intelligence processes this data continuously, identifying road signs, pedestrians, and nearby vehicles. Although these systems can assist with driving tasks, human oversight remains essential for safety and decision-making.

Artificial Narrow Intelligence also improves transportation safety by predicting risks before accidents occur. Driver-assistance technologies monitor lane position, detect obstacles, and apply emergency braking when necessary. Similar predictive systems are used in aviation and rail networks to detect equipment problems and prevent mechanical failures before they become dangerous.

Beyond individual vehicles, ANI supports global logistics and supply chains. Shipping companies, airlines, and trucking networks use AI systems to optimize routes, reduce fuel consumption, and improve delivery schedules. These technologies allow goods to move more efficiently across international markets.

Public transportation systems also benefit from intelligent technologies. By analyzing passenger demand and travel patterns, ANI helps city planners adjust schedules, manage traffic flow, and reduce congestion. These improvements make urban transportation more reliable and accessible for growing populations.

Finally, the chapter highlighted environmental benefits and ethical considerations related to AI in transportation. Intelligent systems can reduce fuel usage and emissions by optimizing traffic patterns and improving route efficiency. However, issues such as data privacy, system reliability, and accountability must be carefully addressed as transportation technologies become increasingly automated.

Overall, Artificial Narrow Intelligence is helping create transportation systems that are safer, smarter, and more sustainable while still relying on human guidance and oversight.

Reflection Section

Transportation systems influence nearly every aspect of modern life. From daily commutes to international shipping, the movement of people and goods supports economic activity and social connection. Artificial Narrow Intelligence has introduced new ways to manage these systems by analyzing data and predicting patterns that improve efficiency and safety.

Students should consider how intelligent technologies are shaping the way people travel. Navigation apps, driver-assistance systems, and automated scheduling tools all rely on AI to process real-time information and guide decisions. These tools make transportation more efficient, but they also require responsible oversight to ensure safety and ethical use.

Another important aspect of AI in transportation is environmental impact. By optimizing routes and reducing traffic congestion, intelligent systems can help reduce fuel consumption and greenhouse gas emissions. This shows how technological innovation can contribute to environmental sustainability.

Reflect on the following questions:

How does Artificial Narrow Intelligence improve transportation safety?

Why is data important for managing modern transportation systems?

How can AI technologies help reduce traffic congestion in cities?

What environmental benefits can result from intelligent transportation systems?

Why must humans remain responsible for overseeing automated transportation technologies?

Student Worksheet

Understanding ANI in Transportation

Part A – Vocabulary Practice

Write a definition in your own words for each of the following terms.

Artificial Narrow Intelligence

Smart Mobility

Autonomous Vehicles

Predictive Maintenance

Transportation Logistics

Sustainable Transportation

Part B – Understanding the Concepts

Answer the following questions using complete sentences.

How does Artificial Narrow Intelligence help manage traffic in modern cities?

What technologies allow self-driving vehicles to detect their surroundings?

Why is predictive safety important in transportation systems?

How does AI help manage global supply chains and logistics?

Why is human oversight still necessary when using automated transportation technologies?

Part C – Real-World Application

Think about technologies that assist transportation in everyday life.

Identify two examples of transportation technologies that may use Artificial Narrow Intelligence and explain how they improve travel or safety.

Example 1:

How it helps transportation systems:

Example 2:

How it helps transportation systems:

Part D – Critical Thinking

Artificial Narrow Intelligence can improve safety and efficiency in transportation systems, but it cannot replace human judgment completely.

Write one paragraph explaining why humans must continue to supervise and guide AI-powered transportation technologies.

Chapter Quiz

ANI in Transportation

Multiple Choice

Artificial Narrow Intelligence improves transportation primarily by:

A. Eliminating vehicles
B. Analyzing data to improve safety and efficiency
C. Replacing all drivers immediately
D. Removing traffic laws

Self-driving vehicles rely on which technologies to understand their surroundings?

A. Cameras, sensors, and GPS systems
B. Paper maps and human memory
C. Mechanical gears only
D. Printed schedules

One benefit of AI in transportation is:

A. Increasing traffic congestion
B. Improving route planning and reducing delays
C. Eliminating public transportation
D. Removing the need for navigation

Predictive maintenance in transportation helps by:

A. Ignoring mechanical problems
B. Detecting potential equipment failures before they occur
C. Eliminating vehicle inspections
D. Reducing the need for safety systems

Why must humans remain involved in transportation systems that use AI?

A. Because AI cannot process data
B. Because human judgment and ethical decisions are still necessary
C. Because machines cannot operate vehicles
D. Because transportation technology cannot improve

Short Answer

Explain one way Artificial Narrow Intelligence helps improve road safety.

Give one example of how AI improves global transportation logistics.

Why can intelligent transportation systems help protect the environment?

Quiz Answer Key

Multiple Choice Answers

B – Analyzing data to improve safety and efficiency

A – Cameras, sensors, and GPS systems

B – Improving route planning and reducing delays

B – Detecting potential equipment failures before they occur

B – Because human judgment and ethical decisions are still necessary

Short Answer Sample Responses

AI systems monitor road conditions, detect obstacles, and provide driver-assistance features such as automatic braking or lane guidance.

AI helps logistics companies analyze shipping routes, track cargo, and schedule deliveries efficiently.

Intelligent transportation systems reduce fuel consumption and emissions by optimizing routes and minimizing traffic congestion.

CHAPTER 8: ANI in Communication — How Machines Connect Humanity

Introduction

Communication is the bridge that connects human minds.
It allows us to share knowledge, express emotion, and build understanding across time and distance. For thousands of years, language and writing have been humanity's most powerful tools for connection.
Now, in the age of Artificial Narrow Intelligence (ANI), machines have begun to assist in this ancient task — helping people speak, translate, and understand one another across cultures and continents.

In this chapter, we will explore how ANI systems power the modern world of communication — from digital translators and virtual assistants to smart customer service chatbots and social media filters. These intelligent systems are not replacing human conversation; rather, they are extending its reach, making it possible for billions of people to connect instantly, regardless of language or location.

The Evolution of Communication

For most of history, communication was limited by distance and language barriers. Letters took days or weeks to arrive. Messages could be misunderstood or lost in translation.
The invention of the telephone, radio, and internet changed that, compressing time and space into seconds. But even with these technologies, understanding remained a challenge — words still had to be translated, tones interpreted, and meanings clarified.

Artificial Narrow Intelligence became the next great leap in this story.
By analyzing enormous datasets of human speech, writing, and images, ANI learned to understand how people express meaning. It can now translate languages instantly, summarize long texts, and even recognize emotion in a person's voice.

In this new era, communication is no longer confined by human speed. It flows through networks of intelligent machines that process words, gestures, and symbols in real time, making the world smaller and more connected than ever before.

Language Translation — Breaking the Boundaries of Words

One of ANI's most visible and inspiring achievements is real-time translation.
In the past, people needed human translators to communicate across languages. Today, systems powered by ANI can listen to speech in one language and immediately reproduce it in another — with remarkable accuracy.

These translation tools are built on deep learning algorithms that have been trained on millions of sentences in dozens of languages. They study grammar, syntax, and tone, learning not just what words mean but how they are used in context.

For example, when someone says "It's raining cats and dogs," an ANI translator knows this phrase doesn't refer to animals falling from the sky — it recognizes it as an idiom meaning

heavy rain.
This subtlety makes modern translation systems feel almost human.

In classrooms, such tools allow students from different backgrounds to learn together. In hospitals, they help doctors communicate with patients who speak other languages. And in international business, they remove barriers that once divided markets.
Through ANI, language is no longer a wall but a bridge.

Voice Recognition and Virtual Assistants

When you speak to a device and it responds — whether answering a question, sending a message, or playing a song — you are interacting with ANI.
Voice assistants like Siri, Alexa, and Google Assistant rely on advanced speech recognition models to understand human language. These systems convert sound waves into digital patterns, recognize words, and interpret commands in fractions of a second.

This process involves several stages: listening, interpreting, responding, and learning. Each time the system hears a phrase, it improves its understanding of accents, tone, and context.
For students, this means easier access to information through simple voice commands. For teachers, it offers tools for organizing lessons, setting reminders, or even assisting students with reading and pronunciation.

Although these assistants are efficient, they lack emotion and comprehension. They can respond logically but not empathetically. This limitation reminds users that while ANI can facilitate conversation, true communication still requires the warmth of human connection.

Chatbots and Customer Interaction

In modern businesses, ANI plays a vital role in communication between companies and customers. Chatbots — automated text-based assistants — handle millions of conversations every day.
They can answer questions, provide recommendations, and even solve simple problems instantly, without human delay.

For example, a student visiting a university website might ask a chatbot about admission deadlines. Within seconds, the system retrieves the correct answer from its database. The exchange feels natural because the chatbot uses human-like language patterns learned from countless interactions.

In classrooms, chatbots can also serve as virtual tutors, guiding students through exercises and answering common questions about assignments.
This ability to hold meaningful dialogue — even within narrow boundaries — demonstrates ANI's growing role as a communicator in both education and everyday life.

Emotion Detection and Sentiment Analysis

While ANI cannot *feel* emotions, it can recognize them.
By analyzing tone of voice, facial expressions, and word choice, intelligent systems can estimate how a person feels — happy, sad, frustrated, or calm.

This capability, called **sentiment analysis**, is widely used in communication systems. Customer service tools can detect when a user is upset and alert a human representative. Social media platforms analyze public emotion to understand how people respond to global events or products.

In mental health apps, ANI models listen to a user's speech for signs of anxiety or depression, offering helpful resources or suggesting professional contact.
Though still imperfect, these systems mark a major step toward technology that listens not just to words, but to the *feelings behind them.*

Information Overload and the Need for Clarity

In the digital age, people are surrounded by information — messages, notifications, posts, and videos that compete for attention every second.
ANI helps manage this overwhelming flow by filtering, summarizing, and prioritizing communication.

Email systems sort important messages automatically. Social media platforms use ANI to recommend relevant content based on user interests. News aggregators summarize articles into concise points, helping readers understand complex events quickly.

However, this convenience comes with responsibility. Algorithms can also create "echo chambers," where people only see information that agrees with their beliefs.
Teachers and students must therefore learn *critical digital literacy* — the ability to question, analyze, and verify what they read online. Technology delivers information, but human wisdom must interpret it.

Global Connectivity and Cultural Exchange

Through ANI-driven communication tools, people are now connecting across cultures like never before. Students in Fiji can attend lectures in London. Musicians in Africa can collaborate with composers in Japan. Scientists from different countries can share data instantly, accelerating discovery.

This global dialogue enriches humanity, turning the world into one vast classroom of ideas.
Each message, translated and transmitted through ANI, carries not just data but the possibility of understanding — proving that technology, when guided by empathy, can unite rather than divide.

Ethical Dimensions of AI Communication

Despite its benefits, ANI in communication raises deep ethical concerns.
When machines analyze our words, voices, and emotions, questions of privacy and trust arise.

Who owns the data we share with voice assistants? How are our messages stored, interpreted, or used?

Transparency and consent are essential. Students and teachers must understand that behind every smart device is a system that learns from human input.
Education about responsible communication — knowing when to trust a machine and when to rely on human judgment — is critical for the next generation of digital citizens.

Conclusion

Artificial Narrow Intelligence has reshaped the way humanity communicates.
It breaks language barriers, simplifies information exchange, and connects people across every border.
Yet amid all this technological brilliance, the essence of communication remains profoundly human — empathy, respect, and shared understanding.

ANI can carry a message, but only humans can give it meaning.
By learning how intelligent systems transmit our voices and words, students and teachers not only master a tool — they rediscover the power of communication itself.
When guided by integrity and compassion, ANI becomes not just a transmitter of data, but a messenger of unity for the entire world.

CHAPTER 8 – TEACHER & STUDENT MATERIALS

Based on "ANI in Communication — How Machines Connect Humanity")

Summary

Artificial Narrow Intelligence (ANI) has transformed how people communicate across the world. In the past, communication was limited by distance and language, but today, intelligent systems allow instant connection regardless of location or language.

ANI powers tools such as language translators, voice assistants, chatbots, and sentiment analysis systems. These technologies help people understand each other, access information quickly, and interact more efficiently in everyday life, education, and business.

Translation systems break language barriers, while voice recognition allows users to interact with devices naturally. Chatbots support communication in customer service and learning environments, and sentiment analysis helps detect emotions in speech and text.

However, the rise of ANI also introduces challenges, including information overload, privacy concerns, and the risk of biased or filtered information. As a result, students must develop digital literacy skills to critically evaluate information.

Ultimately, while ANI enhances communication, human qualities such as empathy, understanding, and ethical judgment remain essential. ANI can deliver messages, but humans give them meaning.

Reflection

How has technology changed the way you communicate with others compared to the past?

Have you ever used a translator or voice assistant? What was your experience?

Why is it important to understand both the benefits and risks of AI communication tools?

How can students make sure they are not misled by information online?

In your opinion, what role should humans play in communication when AI is involved?

Worksheet

Part A: Vocabulary Matching

Match the term with its correct definition:

A. Language Translation
B. Chatbot
C. Sentiment Analysis
D. Voice Recognition
E. Digital Literacy

___ Ability of a system to understand spoken words

___ AI system that analyzes emotions in text or speech

___ AI tool that converts one language into another

___ Automated system that communicates with users through text

___ Skill of evaluating and understanding online information

Part B: Short Answer

What is Artificial Narrow Intelligence (ANI)?

Give one example of how ANI helps in education.

Why are chatbots useful in businesses or schools?

What is one risk of relying too much on AI communication tools?

How does ANI help reduce language barriers?

Part C: Critical Thinking

Write a short paragraph (5–7 sentences):

Explain how ANI can both improve and challenge human communication.

Quiz (10 Questions)

Multiple Choice

What does ANI stand for?
A. Artificial Natural Intelligence
B. Artificial Narrow Intelligence
C. Automated Neural Interface
D. Advanced Network Intelligence

What is one main benefit of ANI in communication?
A. It replaces all human interaction
B. It slows down communication
C. It helps people connect globally
D. It eliminates the need for language

Which tool helps convert speech into text?
A. Chatbot
B. Translator
C. Voice Recognition
D. Sentiment Analyzer

What is the purpose of sentiment analysis?
A. To translate languages
B. To detect emotions
C. To store data
D. To send messages

Chatbots are mainly used for:
A. Cooking food
B. Managing conversations automatically
C. Driving cars
D. Creating hardware

What is a risk of AI-powered communication systems?
A. Faster responses

B. Better translations
C. Privacy concerns
D. Improved learning

What does digital literacy help students do?
A. Build computers
B. Analyze and evaluate information
C. Replace teachers
D. Avoid technology

ANI systems learn from:
A. Random guessing
B. Human data and patterns
C. Only images
D. Hardware chips

What is one limitation of voice assistants?
A. They are too slow
B. They cannot process language
C. They lack emotional understanding
D. They cannot access the internet

According to the chapter, communication is ultimately:
A. Fully controlled by machines
B. Completely automated
C. A human-centered process
D. Unnecessary

Answer Key

Worksheet Answers

Part A:

D

C

A

B

E

Part B (Sample Answers):

ANI is a type of AI designed to perform specific tasks.

It helps students translate languages or access information using voice assistants.

Chatbots provide instant responses and support communication.

One risk is over-reliance or loss of privacy.

It translates languages instantly, allowing people to understand each other.

Quiz Answers

B

C

C

B

B

C

B

B

C

C

CHAPTER 9 ANI in Business and Finance — How Smart Systems Shape the Global Economy

Introduction

Business is the engine of the global economy — the system through which ideas become products, services, and opportunities.
Finance, in turn, is its bloodstream, circulating money, data, and decisions through every corner of society.
In the twenty-first century, both of these forces are being transformed by **Artificial Narrow Intelligence (ANI)**.

From banks that detect fraud in seconds to online shops that predict what customers want before they ask, ANI has become an invisible worker in the world of commerce.
It analyzes transactions, manages risk, personalizes marketing, and automates millions of small decisions that once required human time and attention.
This chapter reveals how narrow intelligence operates inside the vast networks of business and finance, showing how it creates efficiency, challenges ethics, and reshapes the meaning of work itself.

The Data-Driven Marketplace

Every modern business is built on information.
Customer preferences, sales patterns, and market trends form the foundation of decision-making.
Before the rise of ANI, companies relied on spreadsheets, surveys, and intuition to plan their strategies. Today, intelligent algorithms analyze billions of data points in real time — revealing connections too subtle for the human mind to notice.

An online store, for instance, learns from each customer's browsing history, identifying products they are most likely to purchase.
Streaming services examine viewing habits to recommend shows.
Banks monitor spending behavior to understand lifestyle patterns and assess credit risk.

Through these data-driven insights, ANI turns raw numbers into predictions.
It allows businesses to anticipate rather than react — a fundamental shift from guesswork to guided intelligence.

Automation and Efficiency

One of the greatest gifts of ANI to business is **automation**.
Repetitive tasks that once consumed hours of human labor can now be performed in moments.
Accounting systems reconcile invoices automatically; inventory software restocks shelves before supplies run out; digital assistants schedule meetings and draft correspondence.

In large corporations, automation powered by ANI reduces operational costs and minimizes human error.
In small businesses, it allows owners to focus on creativity, innovation, and customer relationships instead of paperwork.

However, this efficiency also raises questions about employment.
As machines handle more tasks, workers must adapt by developing skills that require empathy, imagination, and critical thinking — qualities beyond the reach of narrow intelligence.

Financial Forecasting and Risk Management

In the financial world, timing and accuracy are everything.
Markets shift by the second, influenced by global events, politics, and emotion.
ANI tools help analysts interpret this chaos. They track stock movements, interest rates, and economic indicators across continents, identifying patterns that signal opportunity or danger.

Banks use ANI to predict loan defaults, manage investment portfolios, and balance risk.
Insurance companies employ similar systems to estimate the likelihood of accidents or natural disasters.
By modeling countless scenarios, these algorithms create a digital simulation of the financial world — a living map that guides decision-makers toward stability.

Yet, behind every model remains human judgment.
A machine can calculate probability, but only a human can weigh ethics, responsibility, and compassion in financial choices that affect people's lives.

Fraud Detection and Cybersecurity

Every transaction in the digital age carries a trace — a sequence of numbers, locations, and timestamps.
ANI excels at detecting patterns that deviate from the norm.
If a credit card normally used in California is suddenly charged in another country within minutes, the system alerts security teams instantly.

Banks rely on these intelligent safeguards to prevent theft and protect customers.
Cybersecurity networks also use ANI to monitor digital traffic, recognizing suspicious behavior before an attack occurs.
This constant vigilance is essential in a world where commerce moves at the speed of light and trust is built on data integrity.

Customer Experience and Personalization

Beyond security and efficiency, ANI has transformed how businesses interact with people.
Through customer relationship platforms, it studies preferences, purchase histories, and even emotions expressed in feedback.
With this knowledge, companies craft personalized experiences — recommending products, sending tailored messages, and predicting needs before they arise.

When used responsibly, personalization feels like service. When misused, it can feel like surveillance.
This delicate balance between convenience and privacy is one of the defining ethical challenges of modern business.
Teachers can help students understand that intelligent technology must always respect human dignity, even when it serves profit.

E-Commerce and Global Reach

Online marketplaces have become global villages of trade.
From a small artisan selling crafts to a multinational company shipping products worldwide, ANI enables fair competition by providing access to tools once reserved for large corporations.

Logistics algorithms optimize delivery routes, translation systems localize websites, and chatbots provide 24-hour customer service.
A single entrepreneur can now operate a digital store serving customers across continents — guided by the same intelligence that drives international giants.

This democratization of commerce shows the creative potential of ANI when combined with human vision.

Ethical and Economic Challenges

Despite its benefits, the use of ANI in business and finance raises important moral questions.
If algorithms determine who receives loans, how do we ensure they are free from bias?
If machines trade billions in seconds, what happens when systems fail or markets crash?

Ethics in AI requires transparency — understanding how decisions are made and who is accountable.
Economic policy must also evolve to support workers whose roles are changing under automation.
Rather than resisting the rise of intelligent systems, education must prepare students to lead them — to become designers, analysts, and innovators who use technology for social good.

The Future of Work

As ANI continues to integrate into business, the nature of work itself is being reimagined.
Future offices will blend human and machine collaboration, where employees work alongside digital assistants that handle routine tasks while humans focus on creativity, empathy, and strategic thinking.

Lifelong learning will become essential.
Students of today will need not only technical skills but also moral literacy — the ability to understand both the power and the limits of intelligent tools.
In this sense, the workforce of tomorrow will not compete with ANI; it will *co-evolve* with it.

Conclusion

Artificial Narrow Intelligence is quietly rewriting the rules of business and finance.
It moves money, manages risk, protects consumers, and personalizes experience.
Yet its true value lies not only in profit or speed but in partnership — a collaboration between human purpose and machine precision.

The businesses that will thrive in the future are those that remember this balance: machines calculate, but humans care; algorithms analyze, but people create meaning.
For students and teachers, this understanding is the foundation of ethical entrepreneurship in the age of intelligence.

When guided by wisdom, ANI does not merely serve the economy — it serves humanity.

CHAPTER 9 – TEACHER & STUDENT MATERIALS

(Based on "ANI in Business and Finance — How Smart Systems Shape the Global Economy")

Summary

Artificial Narrow Intelligence (ANI) plays a powerful role in modern business and finance by helping organizations make faster, smarter, and more accurate decisions. In today's data-driven world, companies rely on ANI to analyze large amounts of information, identify patterns, and predict outcomes.

ANI supports businesses in several ways, including automation of routine tasks, improving efficiency, and reducing human error. In finance, it helps forecast market trends, manage risks, and detect fraud in real time. Banks and companies use ANI systems to monitor transactions and protect customers from cyber threats.

Additionally, ANI enhances customer experience through personalization, recommending products and services based on user behavior. It also supports global commerce by enabling businesses of all sizes to reach customers worldwide.

However, the use of ANI raises important ethical and economic challenges, such as concerns about privacy, bias, and job displacement. As technology continues to evolve, students must understand both its benefits and limitations.

Ultimately, the future of business will depend on collaboration between humans and intelligent systems, where machines handle data and efficiency while humans provide creativity, empathy, and ethical judgment.

Reflection

How has technology changed the way businesses operate today?

What are some ways ANI helps companies make better decisions?

Do you think automation is helpful or harmful to workers? Why?

How can businesses balance personalization with customer privacy?

What skills do you think future workers will need in an AI-driven economy?

Worksheet

Part A: Vocabulary Matching

Match each term with its correct definition:

A. Automation
B. Fraud Detection
C. Personalization
D. Financial Forecasting
E. Cybersecurity

___ Protecting systems and data from digital threats

___ Predicting future financial trends using data

___ Using machines to perform tasks automatically

___ Identifying suspicious or illegal financial activity

___ Customizing services based on user preferences

Part B: Short Answer

What is Artificial Narrow Intelligence (ANI)?

How does ANI improve efficiency in businesses?

Give one example of how ANI is used in finance.

Why is fraud detection important in modern banking?

What is one ethical concern related to ANI in business?

Part C: Critical Thinking

Write a paragraph (5–7 sentences):

Explain how ANI is changing the future of work and what students should do to prepare for it.

Quiz (10 Questions)

Multiple Choice

What does ANI stand for?
A. Artificial Natural Intelligence
B. Artificial Narrow Intelligence
C. Automated Network Intelligence
D. Advanced Neural Integration

What is a key role of ANI in business?

A. Replacing all human workers
B. Analyzing data to support decisions
C. Eliminating technology
D. Slowing down processes

What does automation help businesses do?
A. Increase manual labor
B. Reduce efficiency

C. Perform repetitive tasks quickly
D. Avoid using technology

What is financial forecasting?
A. Recording past transactions
B. Predicting future financial trends
C. Creating advertisements
D. Selling products online

How does ANI help detect fraud?
A. By ignoring transactions
B. By recognizing unusual patterns
C. By slowing down payments
D. By blocking all users

What is personalization in business?
A. Treating all customers the same
B. Customizing services for each customer
C. Removing customer data
D. Avoiding communication

What is one ethical concern of ANI?
A. Faster processing
B. Lower costs
C. Privacy and bias
D. Better customer service

How does ANI support global commerce?
A. By limiting trade
B. By increasing language barriers
C. By enabling worldwide online business
D. By reducing communication

What type of skills will future workers need?
A. Only physical labor skills
B. No new skills
C. Creativity and critical thinking
D. Less education

What is the main idea of the chapter?
A. Technology replaces humans completely
B. ANI improves business but requires human responsibility
C. Business no longer needs people
D. Finance is not important

Answer Key

Worksheet Answers

Part A:

E

D

A

B

C

Part B (Sample Answers):

ANI is AI designed to perform specific tasks.

It automates tasks and reduces human error.

It helps detect fraud or predict market trends.

It protects customers and prevents financial loss.

Bias, privacy concerns, or job displacement.

Quiz Answers

B

B

C

B

B

B

C

C

C

B

CHAPTER 10: ANI in Entertainment and Media — How Machines Shape Creativity and Culture

Introduction

Art, music, stories, and performance have always been at the heart of human culture.
They are how we express emotion, share identity, and pass knowledge from one generation to the next.
For centuries, creativity seemed like the one domain that belonged entirely to humans — the realm of imagination, intuition, and feeling.
But in the twenty-first century, **Artificial Narrow Intelligence (ANI)** has entered this space too.

Today, algorithms compose music, write movie scripts, edit videos, design game levels, and even create digital paintings.
This chapter explores how ANI supports creativity — not by replacing human artists, but by expanding the boundaries of what they can do. It also examines the ethical questions that arise when machines participate in art, and the importance of keeping the human spirit at the center of culture.

The Evolution of Creative Technology

The relationship between art and technology is not new.
From the invention of the camera to digital recording, every tool has changed how artists work.
ANI represents the next stage of that evolution — a creative partner built from data and algorithms.

Early music generators in the 1980s could compose simple melodies by following mathematical rules.
Today's systems, powered by deep learning, study thousands of compositions, learning rhythm, harmony, and mood.
When asked to create, they produce entirely new arrangements that sound surprisingly human.

In film production, ANI tools edit scenes automatically, balance color, and even suggest camera angles based on emotional tone.
Writers use intelligent text generators to overcome creative blocks, brainstorm ideas, or improve dialogue.
Artists use neural networks to transform sketches into photorealistic images, blending technology and imagination into something uniquely modern.

Music and Sound

One of the earliest and most profound uses of ANI in entertainment is in **music creation**. Algorithms can now analyze decades of recordings to identify what makes a song popular — tempo, melody, key, or emotional energy.
Based on this knowledge, systems generate new songs or assist composers in writing harmonies.

Streaming platforms like Spotify and Apple Music use ANI to recommend tracks that fit a listener's taste. By studying user behavior — what songs are skipped, replayed, or saved — these systems learn individual preferences and craft personalized playlists.

In the recording studio, producers rely on AI-driven tools to clean up audio, adjust pitch, and match instruments.
Yet, even with all this innovation, the soul of music remains human.
The machine can suggest notes and rhythms, but it cannot feel the heartbreak behind a love song or the triumph behind an anthem. Emotion still belongs to the artist.

Film, Animation, and Visual Arts

The film and television industries have embraced ANI as a creative collaborator.
Editing software now uses intelligent algorithms to organize footage, detect scenes, and even recommend the most engaging cuts.
In animation, ANI systems generate facial expressions and movement, saving artists hours of manual work while maintaining lifelike realism.

Special effects studios use machine learning to simulate explosions, weather, or entire landscapes.
What once took weeks of rendering now happens in hours.
By automating the technical side, ANI gives filmmakers more freedom to focus on storytelling — the human heart of every production.

In visual arts, neural networks known as **generative adversarial networks (GANs)** create original digital paintings by studying millions of artistic styles. Some of these AI artworks have even been displayed in galleries and sold at major auctions.
This sparks an important classroom discussion: when a machine makes art, who is the true artist — the programmer, the algorithm, or the idea itself?

Gaming and Interactive Media

Video games are among the most complex and immersive forms of entertainment, and ANI plays a vital role in bringing them to life.
Game engines use intelligent systems to design virtual environments that react dynamically to player actions.
Enemies adapt their strategies, non-player characters (NPCs) respond with realistic behavior, and difficulty levels adjust automatically based on performance.

ANI also generates landscapes, quests, and dialogue, ensuring that no two playthroughs are exactly alike.
This transforms gaming from a scripted experience into a living, interactive story.

For educational games, ANI personalizes challenges according to each student's learning progress, turning play into a powerful form of education.
Through these innovations, entertainment becomes more than fun — it becomes a pathway for exploration, problem-solving, and imagination.

Journalism and Media Production

The world of journalism has also felt the influence of Artificial Narrow Intelligence.
Automated writing systems generate weather reports, sports summaries, and stock market updates in real time.
News organizations use ANI to detect breaking stories, verify facts, and even identify misinformation spreading online.

In broadcasting, intelligent editing tools caption videos, translate live content, and recommend stories to viewers based on their interests.
Social media platforms rely on AI-driven algorithms to decide which content appears on users' feeds, shaping global conversations every second.

While these systems make communication faster and more efficient, they also carry responsibility.
Teachers can guide students to ask: Who decides what we see? How do algorithms shape our opinions?
Learning to question technology is as important as learning to use it.

The Creative Partnership

The most exciting vision of ANI in entertainment is one of **collaboration**.
Humans provide imagination and emotion; machines provide speed and analysis. Together, they form a new kind of creative team.

A filmmaker might ask an ANI tool to generate hundreds of visual concepts for a futuristic city, then choose the one that inspires their artistic vision.
A composer might feed an AI the sound of rain, asking it to build harmonies from nature's rhythm.
In classrooms, students can experiment with AI art tools to explore their own creativity while learning about how technology interprets beauty.

The partnership between artist and algorithm challenges a powerful myth — that machines destroy creativity.
In truth, they expand it, offering humans new ways to imagine, invent, and express.

Ethics and the Future of Creativity

As with every use of ANI, creativity also brings ethical concerns.
If a song or painting is created by a machine, who owns the copyright?
If an algorithm reproduces a human artist's style, is that imitation or theft?
And what happens when artificial systems produce content so realistic that it becomes difficult to distinguish from reality — as in the case of "deepfake" videos?

These questions remind us that creativity is not only about output, but also about responsibility. Teachers and students must learn to see ANI not as an all-knowing artist, but as a tool whose use must be guided by integrity, empathy, and respect for original work.

Culture in the Age of Intelligence

Culture is more than entertainment — it is the story of who we are.
ANI is now helping preserve endangered languages, digitize ancient art, and restore damaged historical recordings.
By analyzing data from museums, archives, and libraries, AI systems bring the past to life for future generations.

At the same time, culture continues to evolve.
Digital artists, musicians, and writers are discovering that collaborating with machines can lead to new forms of expression never before possible.
The challenge is to ensure that technology deepens humanity's voice rather than silencing it.

Conclusion

Artificial Narrow Intelligence has entered the creative world not as a replacement, but as a partner.
It assists musicians in composing, filmmakers in editing, journalists in reporting, and artists in imagining.
Through this collaboration, humanity is learning that creativity is not limited to emotion or code, but to the harmony between them.

The future of entertainment and media belongs to those who can blend human imagination with machine precision — to create art that not only entertains, but also enlightens.

When guided by ethics, empathy, and curiosity, ANI becomes more than technology — it becomes a mirror reflecting the endless creativity of the human spirit.

CHAPTER 10 – TEACHER & STUDENT MATERIALS

(Based on "ANI in Entertainment and Media — How Machines Shape Creativity and Culture")

Summary

Artificial Narrow Intelligence (ANI) is transforming the world of entertainment and media by supporting human creativity in new and powerful ways. While creativity has traditionally been seen as a uniquely human ability, ANI now assists in producing music, films, art, video games, and journalism.

ANI systems analyze large amounts of creative data to generate music, recommend content, edit videos, and design digital artwork. In music, AI helps compose songs and personalize playlists. In film and animation, it improves editing, special effects, and visual storytelling. In gaming, ANI creates dynamic and interactive experiences that adapt to players.

In journalism and media, ANI helps produce real-time reports, detect misinformation, and personalize content for audiences. These tools increase efficiency but also raise important questions about bias, control, and the spread of information.

Despite these advancements, human creativity remains essential. ANI cannot truly feel emotion or understand meaning the way humans do. Instead, it acts as a creative partner, expanding possibilities while relying on human imagination and ethical guidance.

As technology evolves, students must understand both the creative opportunities and ethical responsibilities that come with using AI in media and culture.

Reflection

How has technology changed the way people create and enjoy entertainment?

Do you think AI can be truly creative, or is it only copying human work? Why?

How would you feel if a machine created a song or artwork similar to your own?

What are the risks of AI-generated content like deepfakes?

How can humans ensure that creativity remains meaningful in an AI-driven world?

Worksheet

Part A: Vocabulary Matching

Match each term with its correct definition:

A. Generative AI
B. Personalization
C. Deepfake
D. Animation Automation
E. Creative Collaboration

___ AI working together with humans to create content

___ Technology that creates realistic but fake media content

___ AI that produces new content such as music or images

___ Customizing content based on user preferences

___ Using AI to automate movement and visual effects

Part B: Short Answer

What is Artificial Narrow Intelligence (ANI)?

How does ANI assist musicians or artists?

Give one example of ANI in gaming or film.

Why is human creativity still important even with AI tools?

What is one ethical concern related to AI in media?

Part C: Critical Thinking

Write a paragraph (5–7 sentences):

Explain how ANI can both enhance and challenge creativity in entertainment and media.

Quiz (10 Questions)

Multiple Choice

What does ANI stand for?
A. Artificial Natural Intelligence
B. Artificial Narrow Intelligence
C. Automated Neural Interaction
D. Advanced Network Integration

What role does ANI play in entertainment?
A. Replacing all artists
B. Supporting and enhancing creativity
C. Eliminating storytelling
D. Removing human involvement

How does ANI help in music?
A. By removing all instruments
B. By analyzing patterns and assisting composition
C. By stopping creativity
D. By replacing musicians entirely

What is one use of ANI in film production?
A. Cooking food
B. Editing scenes and creating effects
C. Building hardware
D. Managing finances

What makes video games more interactive using ANI?
A. Fixed storylines
B. Static environments
C. Adaptive characters and environments
D. No player input

What is a deepfake?
A. A type of video game
B. A fake but realistic AI-generated video or image
C. A music style
D. A hardware device

How does ANI affect journalism?
A. Slows down reporting
B. Eliminates news
C. Generates reports and analyzes information
D. Stops communication

What is one ethical concern of AI in media?
A. Faster production
B. Lower costs

C. Ownership and authenticity of content
D. Better quality

Why is human creativity still necessary?
A. Machines cannot process data
B. Machines cannot feel emotion or meaning
C. Machines are too slow
D. Machines cannot generate content

What is the main message of the chapter?
A. AI replaces all creativity
B. Creativity no longer matters
C. AI and humans can work together to create
D. Technology should be avoided

Answer Key

Worksheet Answers

Part A:

E

C

A

B

D

Part B (Sample Answers):

ANI is AI designed to perform specific tasks.

It helps compose music or generate ideas.

It creates adaptive game environments or edits films.

Humans provide emotion, meaning, and originality.

Issues like copyright, deepfakes, or authenticity.

Quiz Answers

B

B

B

B

C

B

C

C

B

C

CHAPTER 11 The Data Behind ANI — Understanding the Power and Purpose of Information

Introduction

At the heart of every intelligent system lies data — streams of numbers, words, sounds, and images that teach machines how to recognize, decide, and act.
Data is the **language of Artificial Narrow Intelligence (ANI)**. It is the raw material from which algorithms learn and the fuel that keeps every digital process alive.

Just as the human brain grows through experience, ANI grows through data. But while humans feel, sense, and remember through living experience, machines absorb information through millions of recorded examples.
This chapter explores what data truly is, how it shapes the behavior of ANI, and why understanding it is essential for teachers and students preparing for the next generation of intelligent systems.

What Is Data?

In its simplest form, **data** is information that can be recorded, measured, and analyzed.
A picture of a flower, a list of temperatures, a patient's heartbeat, or a student's quiz score — all

are forms of data.
When these fragments are organized and interpreted, they reveal patterns that tell a story.

For ANI, data serves as experience. A machine trained on millions of photos learns to recognize objects. Another trained on language samples learns to predict the next word in a sentence. Each piece of information becomes a tiny lesson in the machine's education.
Unlike humans, who need only a few experiences to understand an idea, ANI requires vast quantities of examples — because it learns statistically, not emotionally.

How Machines See the World

Humans see the world through emotion and context; machines see it through numbers.
To a person, a photograph of a sunrise may evoke beauty and warmth. To an ANI system, that same image becomes a grid of pixel values representing color and brightness.
Through training, the system discovers which numeric patterns belong to "sunrises" and which belong to "mountains" or "clouds."

This process transforms the world into a digital landscape — one that ANI can measure, sort, and learn from.
Every sound becomes a waveform, every sentence a sequence of probabilities.
In this transformation, meaning is reduced to form, but through form, the machine begins to *approximate* understanding.

The Journey from Raw Data to Knowledge

The pathway from data to intelligence involves several stages:

1. **Collection:** Information is gathered from sensors, databases, or user input.
2. **Processing:** Data is cleaned, filtered, and organized so the system can interpret it correctly.
3. **Training:** Algorithms study the data, searching for recurring patterns.
4. **Testing:** The system applies what it has learned to new information, measuring accuracy.
5. **Feedback:** Errors are corrected, and the cycle repeats, refining performance.

In classrooms, this can be compared to how students learn. They collect facts, practice with examples, test their understanding, and improve through correction.
In this sense, ANI mirrors the learning cycle of education itself.

Good Data vs. Bad Data

Not all data teaches the right lessons.
If a student studies from incorrect information, they will misunderstand the subject. The same happens with machines.
When data is incomplete, biased, or outdated, the results become misleading.

For example, if an AI for job recruitment is trained mostly on data from one demographic group, it may unintentionally favor that group when evaluating applicants.
This is called **data bias** — a major ethical challenge in modern AI.

Teachers can use this concept to show students why diversity in data matters.
The more varied and balanced the training material, the fairer and more accurate the system becomes.
In this way, building AI is also a lesson in equality and justice.

Big Data and the Digital Revolution

In the early years of computing, data was limited and stored in small files.
Today, the world produces **billions of gigabytes** of new information every day — a phenomenon known as *Big Data*.
Every click, search, purchase, and photo upload adds to this ocean of knowledge.

ANI systems swim in this digital sea. They extract meaning from what seems like chaos — identifying trends in global weather, consumer behavior, public health, and even language evolution.
Through big data, scientists can predict storms, doctors can trace diseases, and teachers can tailor education to individual learning patterns.

However, the more data collected, the greater the need for privacy, security, and ethical use.
Students must learn that in the age of data, knowledge is power — and power must always be handled with care.

Data and Privacy

Every dataset has a human story behind it.
When people share photos, locations, or health information online, that data becomes part of a machine's memory.
Protecting it is essential to preserving trust in technology.

Privacy laws and encryption systems exist to ensure that personal information is stored safely.
But ethical responsibility goes beyond law — it includes empathy.
Developers, teachers, and future leaders must remember that behind every data point is a person who deserves respect.

Teaching digital ethics is therefore as vital as teaching programming. Understanding the moral weight of data helps students grow into responsible creators of technology.

Data as a Shared Resource

The power of ANI lies not only in what it knows but in how knowledge is shared.
When hospitals, universities, and research centers exchange anonymized data, discoveries accelerate.
When governments release open data, communities find new solutions to social challenges.
This cooperative spirit mirrors the best traditions of science and education — learning together for the common good.

By viewing data as a shared resource rather than private treasure, humanity can use ANI to improve lives rather than divide them.
Students who grasp this concept early will become the innovators who use technology to unite the world.

The Ethics of Information

Ethics in data means fairness, honesty, and accountability.
If a system makes a mistake, humans must be able to trace how that decision was made.
Transparency is the foundation of trust between people and machines.

Educators can introduce discussions such as:
Should all data be public?
When does collection become surveillance?
How much should machines know about our private lives?

By engaging with these questions, students learn that technology is not just technical — it is moral, social, and human.

Conclusion

Data is the unseen foundation of Artificial Narrow Intelligence — the invisible ink that writes the story of every algorithm.
It gives machines the ability to perceive, predict, and assist, yet it also carries risk when handled without wisdom.

For teachers, this chapter offers a new way to teach digital literacy: not as a list of rules, but as a study of responsibility.
For students, it offers a glimpse into the language of the future — a language written not in words, but in patterns, numbers, and connections.

When guided by integrity, data becomes more than information; it becomes *understanding*.
And in that understanding lies humanity's greatest opportunity — to build intelligent systems that reflect not only our knowledge, but also our values.

CHAPTER 11 – TEACHER & STUDENT MATERIALS

(Based on "The Data Behind ANI — Understanding the Power and Purpose of Information")

Summary

Data is the foundation of Artificial Narrow Intelligence (ANI). It consists of information such as numbers, images, sounds, and text that machines use to learn and make decisions. Just as humans learn from experience, ANI systems learn from large amounts of data.

Machines do not understand the world the same way humans do. Instead of emotions and context, they interpret information as numbers and patterns. Through processes like data collection, processing, training, testing, and feedback, ANI systems improve their performance over time.

The quality of data is extremely important. Good data leads to accurate and fair outcomes, while poor or biased data can result in incorrect or unfair decisions. This makes data ethics and diversity critical in AI development.

In today's digital world, massive amounts of information—known as Big Data—are generated every day. ANI systems use this data to make predictions, improve services, and support decision-making in areas like healthcare, education, and business.

However, with great data comes great responsibility. Issues such as privacy, security, and ethical use must be carefully managed. Students must learn that data represents real people and should be handled with respect.

Ultimately, understanding data is essential for understanding AI, as it shapes how intelligent systems behave and impacts society as a whole.

Reflection

Why is data considered the "fuel" of artificial intelligence?

How do machines "see" the world differently than humans?

Why is it important to use accurate and diverse data?

How does Big Data impact everyday life?

What responsibilities come with collecting and using data?

Worksheet

Part A: Vocabulary Matching

Match each term with its correct definition:

A. Data
B. Big Data
C. Data Bias
D. Data Processing
E. Privacy

___ Protecting personal information from misuse

___ Large amounts of information generated daily

___ Organizing and cleaning information for analysis

___ Unfair or unbalanced information used in AI systems

___ Facts or information used for analysis

Part B: Short Answer

What is data in simple terms?

How do machines learn from data?

What is one example of Big Data in everyday life?

Why is data bias a problem?

How can we protect personal data?

Part C: Critical Thinking

Write a paragraph (5–7 sentences):

Explain why data ethics is important when building and using AI systems.

Quiz (10 Questions)

Multiple Choice

What is data?
A. Only numbers
B. Information that can be recorded and analyzed

C. Only images
D. Only text

How do machines understand the world?
A. Through emotions
B. Through numbers and patterns
C. Through imagination
D. Through feelings

What is the first step in the data learning process?
A. Testing
B. Feedback
C. Collection
D. Training

What is Big Data?
A. Small files
B. Limited information
C. Large amounts of data generated daily
D. Only business data

What happens when AI is trained with biased data?
A. It becomes faster
B. It becomes fairer
C. It produces unfair or inaccurate results
D. Nothing changes

Why is data processing important?
A. It deletes all data
B. It organizes data for better understanding
C. It stops learning
D. It replaces data

What is one concern related to data use?

A. Speed
B. Privacy
C. Color
D. Size

What does data represent in real life?

A. Only machines
B. Only computers
C. Real people and real information
D. Only numbers

Why is sharing data important?

A. It slows progress
B. It helps collaboration and discovery
C. It removes privacy
D. It stops innovation

What is the main message of the chapter?

A. Data is unimportant
B. AI works without data
C. Data is essential and must be used responsibly
D. Data should be ignored

Answer Key

Worksheet Answers

Part A:

E

B

D

C

A

Part B (Sample Answers):

Data is information that can be recorded and analyzed.

Machines learn by analyzing patterns in large datasets.

Social media activity or online shopping data.

It can lead to unfair or incorrect decisions.

By using security measures and respecting privacy laws.

Quiz Answers

B

B

C

C

C

B

B

C

B

C

CHAPTER 12 Ethics and Responsibility in ANI — Teaching Machines to Do Good

Introduction

Artificial Narrow Intelligence is built by human hands and minds.
It learns from the data we feed it and acts according to the goals we set.
Because of this, every decision an intelligent system makes is a reflection of human choices.
If we want machines to do good, we must teach them what *good* means — and that begins with ethics.

This chapter explores how ethics and responsibility guide the development and use of ANI.
Students and teachers will discover that intelligence alone is not enough; wisdom must direct it.
Technology gains purpose only when it serves humanity with fairness, compassion, and respect for life.

What Is Ethics in Artificial Intelligence?

Ethics is the study of right and wrong — the principles that help people decide how to act responsibly.
In Artificial Intelligence, ethics means designing systems that make decisions aligned with human values.
When developers build an ANI system to diagnose disease, predict credit risk, or recommend content, they must consider the impact those choices have on individuals and society.

Ethics in AI asks essential questions:
Is this system fair to everyone?
Does it protect privacy?
Could it harm people, even unintentionally?
These questions shape the moral compass of every intelligent technology.

Why Ethics Matters

Machines may be logical, but they are not moral.
They follow mathematical patterns, not feelings.
An AI that recommends news articles may accidentally spread misinformation; one that screens job applications may reflect hidden social biases.

Ethics matters because it protects human dignity.
It reminds creators that data represents real lives, not just numbers.
It ensures that innovation uplifts communities rather than exploiting them.
Without ethical reflection, intelligence risks becoming power without conscience — efficient but blind to justice.

Bias and Fairness

Bias occurs when an ANI system produces unfair results because of the data it was trained on.
If most examples in a dataset represent one group, the system may learn to favor that group and misjudge others.

For instance, a facial-recognition system trained mainly on lighter-skinned faces may struggle to identify darker-skinned individuals accurately.
This is not because the machine "chooses" to discriminate — it mirrors the imbalance in its training data.

To build fairness into AI, developers must test systems with diverse, inclusive datasets and continually evaluate their performance.
Teachers can use this concept to help students understand that technology is only as just as the humans who create it.
Fair data leads to fair outcomes.

Transparency and Accountability

Transparency means that the actions of an AI system can be explained and understood.
When a machine denies a loan, recommends a video, or flags an email as spam, people should know *why*.

Accountability ensures that when errors occur, someone is responsible for correcting them.
It is not enough to say "the computer decided." Humans must always remain in control.

In classrooms, educators can illustrate this idea through examples.
If an ANI system misclassifies homework, who fixes it? The student, the teacher, or the programmer?
Such discussions teach critical thinking — that responsibility cannot be delegated to code.

Privacy and Consent

In the digital age, data is everywhere: in phones, cameras, health records, and classroom apps.
Each piece of data tells a story about someone's life.
Ethical AI development requires permission, protection, and respect.

Students should learn that when they share information online, they are contributing to a larger network of learning systems.
Understanding privacy builds awareness and empowerment.
It reminds future innovators that trust is earned when users know how their data is collected, stored, and used.

Environmental Responsibility

Ethics also includes care for the planet.
Training and running ANI systems require energy and computing power.
Designing efficient algorithms and using renewable energy help reduce the environmental footprint of AI.
Teachers can link this topic to sustainability lessons, showing that intelligence extends beyond machines — it includes caring for the Earth that sustains them.

The Human in the Loop

No matter how advanced ANI becomes, a human must remain in the loop.
This phrase means that humans oversee, guide, and correct the system's actions.
In medicine, a doctor reviews AI diagnoses; in finance, an analyst approves automated decisions.

Keeping humans involved ensures that compassion and context remain central.
Machines can process facts, but only humans can weigh feelings, ethics, and consequences.

Teaching Ethics in Schools

Ethics education begins long before students become engineers.
In classrooms, discussions about fairness, privacy, and honesty prepare young minds to use technology responsibly.
Teachers can encourage students to analyze case studies where AI made mistakes and explore how those errors could be prevented.

By connecting ethics to everyday life — social media use, online behavior, and respect for others — students learn that morality is not a separate subject.
It is the foundation of all intelligent action.

Global Guidelines and Shared Values

Nations and organizations around the world are developing ethical frameworks for AI.
Documents such as the **UNESCO Recommendation on the Ethics of Artificial Intelligence** emphasize human rights, inclusion, and accountability.
Although cultures differ, a common principle unites them: technology must serve humanity, not control it.

By studying these global efforts, students gain a sense of shared responsibility — that building ethical AI is a universal mission, connecting classrooms in every country.

The Future of Ethical Intelligence

As ANI evolves, so will the questions it raises.
Can machines ever understand morality?
Should robots have rights?
How do we balance innovation with safety?

Such questions invite philosophical exploration and civic dialogue.
They show that the story of AI is not just scientific — it is human.
By teaching students to think ethically today, we ensure that tomorrow's technologies will be guided by conscience, not just code.

Conclusion

Artificial Narrow Intelligence is powerful, but power without ethics can be dangerous.
Teaching machines to "do good" begins with teaching humans to define what good means.
Fairness, transparency, privacy, and environmental care are not technical options — they are moral obligations.

For teachers, this chapter offers a framework to shape discussions about responsibility in technology.
For students, it plants a seed of awareness: every intelligent system reflects the choices of its creators.

When ethics and intelligence walk hand in hand, machines become partners in progress, not threats to it.
Guided by human values, ANI can help build a future where technology amplifies the best of who we are — wise, compassionate, and just.

CHAPTER 12 – TEACHER & STUDENT MATERIALS

(Ethics and Responsibility in ANI — Teaching Machines to Do Good)

Summary

Ethics in Artificial Narrow Intelligence (ANI) focuses on ensuring that intelligent systems make decisions aligned with human values such as fairness, privacy, and responsibility. Since AI systems learn from human-created data and instructions, their behavior reflects human choices.

Ethics is important because machines are not capable of moral reasoning. Without guidance, AI systems can unintentionally spread bias, misinformation, or unfair outcomes. Issues such as data bias, privacy concerns, and lack of transparency highlight the need for ethical oversight.

Key principles include fairness (avoiding bias), transparency (understanding how decisions are made), accountability (humans remain responsible), and privacy (protecting personal data). Environmental responsibility is also important due to the energy used by AI systems.

The concept of keeping a "human in the loop" ensures that humans supervise AI decisions. Education plays a major role in preparing students to think ethically about technology.

Ultimately, ethical AI depends on human values. When guided by fairness and compassion, ANI can benefit society and support a better future.

Reflection

Why is ethics important when developing AI systems?

What is data bias, and why can it be harmful?

How can humans stay responsible for decisions made by AI?

Why is privacy important in the digital age?

How can students apply ethical thinking when using technology?

Worksheet

Part A: Vocabulary Matching

A. Ethics
B. Bias
C. Transparency
D. Accountability
E. Privacy

___ Protecting personal information

___ Being responsible for decisions and outcomes

___ Ability to explain how decisions are made

___ Principles of right and wrong

___ Unfair patterns in data or decisions

Part B: Short Answer

What does ethics mean in AI?

Why can machines make unfair decisions?

What is one example of bias in AI?

What does "human in the loop" mean?

Why should AI systems be transparent?

Part C: Critical Thinking

Write a paragraph (5–7 sentences):

Explain why humans must guide AI systems with ethical values.

Quiz (10 Questions)

What is ethics?
A. A type of machine
B. Study of right and wrong
C. A computer program
D. A data system

Why is ethics important in AI?
A. Machines have emotions
B. Machines need guidance from human values
C. It slows down systems
D. It removes data

What is bias in AI?
A. Faster processing
B. Fair decisions
C. Unfair outcomes due to data
D. Better performance

What does transparency mean?
A. Hiding information
B. Explaining how decisions are made
C. Faster computing
D. Data storage

Who is responsible for AI decisions?
A. Machines
B. Nobody
C. Humans
D. Data

What does privacy protect?
A. Machines
B. Personal information
C. Computers
D. Programs

What is the "human in the loop"?
A. Machines controlling humans

B. Humans supervising AI
C. No human involvement
D. Data storage

What is one ethical concern in AI?
A. Speed
B. Color
C. Bias
D. Size

Why is fairness important?
A. It makes AI faster
B. It ensures equal treatment
C. It reduces cost
D. It removes data

What is the main idea of the chapter?
A. AI should work alone
B. Ethics must guide AI
C. AI replaces humans
D. Ethics is not needed

Answer Key

Worksheet Part A:

E

D

C

A

B

Quiz Answers:

B

B

C

B

C

B

B

C

B

B

CHAPTER 13 Humans and Machines Working Together — The New Partnership of Intelligence

Introduction

Throughout history, every great invention — from the wheel to the computer — has changed not only how humans work, but how they think.
Today, with the rise of **Artificial Narrow Intelligence (ANI)**, that relationship is deepening into something extraordinary: **a partnership between human creativity and machine precision**.

This chapter explores how people and machines now collaborate in classrooms, hospitals, businesses, and homes.
Rather than replacing humans, ANI extends human abilities — turning information into insight, repetition into efficiency, and imagination into innovation.
Together, they are building a new kind of intelligence: one that blends logic with compassion, speed with judgment, and technology with purpose.

From Tools to Teammates

For centuries, machines were simple tools. A hammer amplified strength, a telescope extended vision, and a computer accelerated calculation.
But ANI is more than a tool — it is a **thinking assistant**. It can analyze, predict, and adapt to human needs.

In this partnership, humans remain the architects of purpose.
A teacher uses AI to track student progress but decides how to encourage improvement.
A doctor consults an AI's diagnosis but interprets it through empathy and experience.
An artist uses AI to generate ideas but selects the one that carries emotional truth.

Thus, ANI becomes a **teammate** — one that listens, learns, and collaborates, while humans provide direction and meaning.

The Shared Intelligence Model

When humans and machines work together, they form what educators call a **shared-intelligence model**.
In this model, humans contribute **context, ethics, and creativity**, while ANI provides **analysis, speed, and consistency**.

Imagine a journalist using an AI program to organize thousands of documents. The AI finds patterns; the journalist uncovers the story.
Or consider a student writing a research paper. ANI can gather sources, summarize information, and suggest structure — but it is the student who shapes the argument and adds voice.

This cooperation reflects the ideal balance of modern intelligence: each partner compensates for the other's limits. Machines handle complexity; humans handle conscience.

In Education

In classrooms, ANI enhances both teaching and learning.
Intelligent tutoring systems monitor each student's progress, identifying strengths and weaknesses.
Teachers then interpret this information to adapt instruction, provide encouragement, and foster curiosity.

Group projects can also include human-AI collaboration. Students use AI tools to analyze data for science experiments, translate foreign texts, or design prototypes for engineering challenges. Through these experiences, learners discover that technology is not just a tool but a collaborator — one that empowers them to think more critically and creatively.

Teachers play the vital role of **ethical guides**, ensuring students understand not only *how* to use AI, but *why* it must be used responsibly.

In Healthcare

In medicine, the partnership between humans and machines saves lives every day.
ANI scans medical images, identifies early signs of disease, and alerts doctors to potential risks.
Physicians interpret these results, consider patient history, and decide on the best treatment.

This combination of machine accuracy and human empathy creates a new standard of care.
It shows that progress happens not when one replaces the other, but when both work in harmony — science guided by compassion.

In Business and Industry

In modern workplaces, humans and machines operate side by side.
ANI automates repetitive processes such as inventory management, scheduling, and data entry, allowing employees to focus on problem-solving and innovation.

Managers use predictive analytics to plan efficiently while maintaining the human insight that algorithms cannot replicate — intuition, teamwork, and leadership.

This partnership is changing what it means to work.
Jobs are evolving from tasks of repetition to roles of creativity and coordination.
Workers who understand AI not as competition but as collaboration become the leaders of tomorrow's economy.

In Everyday Life

Beyond offices and laboratories, ANI assists people in daily routines — navigating roads, translating conversations, suggesting recipes, and reminding users to stay healthy.
These interactions may feel ordinary, yet they represent a profound change: humanity is learning to live alongside intelligent systems.

Every "thank you" spoken to a voice assistant or every decision made with an algorithm's help reinforces a new habit — cooperation.
Students should see these moments not as signs of dependence, but as opportunities to practice awareness and digital responsibility.

Trust and Teamwork

No partnership thrives without trust.
Humans must trust that machines will perform reliably, while machines depend on humans for guidance and correction.
This mutual reliance demands **transparency** — clear understanding of how systems make decisions — and **accountability** — human oversight of outcomes.

Just as in a classroom or workplace team, communication between human and machine matters.
People must learn how to give precise instructions, interpret feedback, and evaluate results critically.
The more clearly humans think, the more effectively machines assist.

Learning from Each Other

When humans observe how ANI learns from patterns, they gain insights into their own learning processes.
Students begin to see parallels between algorithms and study habits — repetition, feedback, and improvement through practice.
Likewise, engineers design AI systems inspired by human biology and psychology.

This exchange forms a **loop of learning** — humans teaching machines how to think, and machines teaching humans how to reflect.
Together, they illuminate the mystery of intelligence itself.

Ethical Partnership

Partnership also carries moral duty.
Humans must ensure that collaboration with ANI upholds fairness, respect, and compassion. Technology should strengthen communities, not replace them; empower workers, not exploit them; and enhance education, not overshadow teachers.

Teachers can lead classroom dialogues about real-world examples — when automation helps, when it harms, and how ethics can guide design.
Through such discussions, students learn that intelligence, whether human or artificial, finds its highest purpose in service to others.

The Future of Co-Intelligence

The next era of progress will not belong to machines alone or to humans alone, but to **co-intelligence** — the union of natural and artificial minds working toward shared goals.
Factories will become ecosystems of collaboration.
Schools will teach hybrid thinking that blends logic and empathy.
Governments and scientists will use AI to solve global challenges such as climate change, poverty, and disease.

In this future, success will not be measured by how powerful machines become, but by how wisely humans lead them.

Conclusion

Artificial Narrow Intelligence has ushered in a new chapter in human history — one defined by cooperation rather than competition.
Machines now complement our strengths and compensate for our weaknesses, allowing us to dream bigger and act faster than ever before.

For teachers, this chapter offers a message of hope: education remains the foundation of every partnership.
For students, it presents a vision of empowerment: by understanding how ANI works and by guiding it ethically, they will shape the intelligent world of tomorrow.

Humanity and machines are not rivals.
They are partners in creation — two forms of intelligence learning to think together, work together, and grow together for the good of all.

CHAPTER 13 – TEACHER & STUDENT MATERIALS

(Humans and Machines Working Together — The New Partnership of Intelligence)

Summary

Artificial Narrow Intelligence (ANI) is transforming the relationship between humans and machines into a collaborative partnership. Instead of replacing humans, ANI enhances human abilities by providing speed, accuracy, and data analysis.

In this partnership, humans contribute creativity, ethical judgment, and emotional understanding, while machines provide efficiency and consistency. This shared intelligence model allows both to work together effectively.

ANI is used in many areas such as education, healthcare, business, and everyday life. In classrooms, it helps personalize learning. In healthcare, it supports doctors with diagnosis. In business, it improves productivity by automating routine tasks.

Trust, communication, and ethical responsibility are essential in this partnership. Humans must guide AI systems and ensure they are used responsibly.

The future lies in "co-intelligence," where humans and machines work together to solve global challenges. Success will depend on how well humans lead and collaborate with AI systems.

Reflection

How are machines different from traditional tools today?

What is the shared intelligence model?

How does ANI help in education or healthcare?

Why is trust important in human-AI partnerships?

What skills do students need for the future of AI collaboration?

Worksheet

Part A: Vocabulary Matching

A. Collaboration
B. Automation
C. Shared Intelligence
D. Co-Intelligence
E. Trust

___ Working together effectively

___ Machines performing tasks automatically

___ Partnership between humans and AI

___ Future cooperation between humans and machines

___ Confidence in systems and outcomes

Part B: Short Answer

What is Artificial Narrow Intelligence (ANI)?

How do humans and machines complement each other?

Give one example of ANI in daily life.

Why is trust important in AI systems?

What is co-intelligence?

Part C: Critical Thinking

Write a paragraph (5–7 sentences):

Explain how humans and AI can work together to solve real-world problems.

Quiz (10 Questions)

What is ANI?
A. Human intelligence
B. AI designed for specific tasks
C. A robot
D. A machine tool

What role do humans play in AI partnerships?
A. No role
B. Provide creativity and ethics
C. Only data input
D. Replace machines

What is shared intelligence?
A. Humans working alone
B. Machines working alone
C. Humans and AI working together
D. Data storage

How does ANI help in education?
A. Replaces teachers
B. Personalizes learning

C. Removes learning
D. Stops teaching

What is one benefit of ANI in healthcare?
A. Slows diagnosis
B. Improves detection of diseases
C. Removes doctors
D. Reduces care

What is automation?
A. Manual work
B. Machines performing tasks
C. No technology
D. Slower processes

Why is trust important?
A. It is not important
B. It ensures reliable collaboration
C. It slows systems
D. It removes data

What is co-intelligence?
A. Competition between humans and AI
B. Cooperation between humans and AI
C. Machine control
D. Human control only

What skill is important for future workers?
A. No skills
B. Creativity and critical thinking
C. Only physical labor
D. Avoiding technology

What is the main idea of the chapter?
A. Humans and machines compete
B. Humans and machines collaborate
C. AI replaces humans
D. Technology should be avoided

Answer Key

Worksheet Part A:

A

B

C

D

E

Quiz Answers:

B

B

C

B

B

B

B

B

B

B

CHAPTER 14 The Challenges and Limits of ANI — Understanding Its Boundaries and Weaknesses

Introduction

Every invention, no matter how powerful, carries both strength and limitation.
Artificial Narrow Intelligence (ANI) is no exception.
While it performs tasks with astonishing accuracy — diagnosing diseases, predicting weather, or driving cars — it remains restricted to the boundaries of its programming and data.

This chapter explores the **limits of ANI**, explaining why machines cannot yet think, feel, or reason as humans do.
It also examines the challenges society faces when relying too heavily on technology, and the importance of human wisdom in guiding intelligent systems.
Students and teachers will discover that understanding limitations is not weakness — it is the beginning of deeper learning and responsibility.

The Narrowness of Narrow Intelligence

The word *narrow* in Artificial Narrow Intelligence defines its greatest strength and its greatest constraint.
ANI is trained to perform one specific task — recognizing speech, analyzing patterns, or translating language — but it cannot go beyond that purpose.

For example, a voice assistant can answer questions but cannot drive a car; a medical algorithm can detect tumors but cannot compose music.
Each system is a specialist, not a generalist.
This is because ANI does not truly "understand" what it is doing — it follows patterns in data rather than forming awareness.

Unlike human intelligence, which adapts fluidly to new situations, ANI must be retrained or redesigned whenever its environment changes.
It lacks common sense, emotion, and self-awareness — qualities that make human thinking flexible and moral.

Dependence on Data

Data is both the foundation and the limitation of ANI.
A machine learns only from the information it has been given. If that data is incomplete, outdated, or biased, its output will be flawed.

Imagine teaching a student only half the alphabet — they could never spell every word correctly.
Similarly, if an AI system for weather prediction is trained only on data from one region, it may fail when applied to another.

Because ANI cannot generate original understanding, it cannot "fill in the blanks" when information is missing.
It learns correlations, not causes; it imitates knowledge without truly grasping meaning.

This dependence on data makes human oversight essential. Teachers can illustrate this point by comparing AI learning to classroom learning: good results depend on the quality of the lessons, not just the quantity.

Lack of True Understanding

While ANI can analyze enormous datasets and detect complex patterns, it does not possess consciousness or comprehension.
It does not "know" what it knows.

For instance, a language model can write essays that sound intelligent, but it does not understand the concepts it describes.
It predicts the next word statistically, not intellectually.
In simple terms, ANI can speak *about* emotion, but it cannot *feel* it.

This absence of understanding becomes critical in sensitive fields such as law, education, and healthcare, where decisions affect real lives.
Only humans can interpret values, ethics, and context — the dimensions of understanding that no algorithm can replicate.

The Problem of Bias

Bias is one of ANI's most serious challenges.
Because machines learn from human-generated data, they often inherit the same prejudices present in society.
A hiring algorithm trained on biased company records might favor certain candidates unfairly.
A criminal prediction system may misjudge communities if its data reflects historical inequality.

These outcomes remind us that technology mirrors humanity's imperfections.
The solution is not to abandon AI but to build it consciously — with diversity, fairness, and continual evaluation.

Students should understand that eliminating bias is not a one-time act but a lifelong commitment to justice in technology.

Vulnerability and Security Risks

Intelligent systems, though powerful, can also be fragile.
Because they depend on digital infrastructure, they are vulnerable to cyberattacks, data corruption, and manipulation.
A single error in code or a breach in security can disrupt entire networks.

For example, if hackers alter an autonomous vehicle's navigation data, the consequences could be catastrophic.
Similarly, misinformation fed into AI-driven communication systems can distort public opinion or spread falsehoods.

Protecting ANI requires constant vigilance — encryption, ethical programming, and human oversight.
As teachers explain these challenges, students can learn that every new technology demands new responsibility.

The Illusion of Perfection

One common misconception is that machines are always correct.
Because AI speaks with confidence, users may assume its answers are infallible.
But ANI can make mistakes — sometimes subtle, sometimes severe.

If an algorithm misreads medical data or misclassifies an image, the outcome can be harmful.
Humans must remember that accuracy does not equal understanding.
Critical thinking — questioning results, verifying sources, and balancing judgment — remains humanity's most essential skill.

In classrooms, this lesson can be taught through reflection: trust technology, but never surrender thought.

Job Displacement and Social Impact

Automation powered by ANI has increased productivity across industries, but it has also changed the nature of work.
Jobs involving routine tasks are increasingly performed by machines, while new roles demand creativity, emotional intelligence, and adaptability.

This shift can cause anxiety about the future of employment. Yet history shows that every technological revolution creates new opportunities.
The challenge for education is to prepare students for roles that blend technical skill with human insight — to become collaborators, not competitors, with machines.

Teachers play a crucial role in guiding this transition, helping students see technology not as a threat, but as a tool for transformation.

Ethical Dilemmas and Responsibility

As ANI systems make decisions once reserved for humans, questions of morality become urgent.
Who is responsible when a self-driving car causes an accident or when a predictive algorithm misjudges a person's potential?

These dilemmas cannot be solved by mathematics alone.
They require empathy, discussion, and shared values — all cultivated through education.

Students who understand ethics today will become the engineers, policymakers, and leaders who design fair and compassionate AI systems tomorrow.

Environmental Cost

Behind every algorithm lies energy consumption.
Training large models requires powerful hardware that uses electricity and resources.
If not managed responsibly, the environmental impact can be significant.

Developers are now exploring ways to make AI more sustainable through efficient coding and renewable energy.
This awareness links digital progress with environmental stewardship — a lesson every future innovator must learn.

Human Supervision — The Final Boundary

The greatest limit of ANI is that it cannot take moral responsibility.
No matter how advanced, it must always remain under human supervision.
Machines can predict, recommend, and automate — but they cannot *decide* in the ethical sense of the word.

Humans must remain the conscience behind the code.
Education ensures that those guiding technology do so with integrity, humility, and compassion.

Conclusion

Artificial Narrow Intelligence is a remarkable achievement, but it operates within boundaries that define its character and control its power.
It cannot feel, imagine, or understand. It cannot replace human wisdom or moral reasoning.

Recognizing these limits is not pessimism — it is maturity.
By studying where ANI stops, humanity learns where it must lead.

For teachers, this chapter encourages balanced dialogue about innovation and responsibility.
For students, it instills the understanding that progress depends not only on smarter machines but on wiser humans.

The lesson is clear: machines may calculate, but only people can care.
And caring — not coding — remains the highest form of intelligence.

CHAPTER 14 – TEACHER & STUDENT MATERIALS

(The Challenges and Limits of ANI — Understanding Its Boundaries and Weaknesses)

Summary

Artificial Narrow Intelligence (ANI) is powerful but limited. It can perform specific tasks with high accuracy, but it cannot think, feel, or understand like humans. Each ANI system is designed for a single purpose and cannot easily adapt to new situations without retraining.

ANI depends heavily on data. If the data is incomplete or biased, the results will also be flawed. Additionally, ANI lacks true understanding—it processes patterns and probabilities but does not comprehend meaning or emotion.

Other challenges include bias, security risks, and the misconception that AI is always correct. Over-reliance on AI can lead to poor decision-making if humans stop thinking critically.

ANI also impacts society by changing jobs and raising ethical questions about responsibility and fairness. Environmental concerns arise due to the energy required to run AI systems.

Ultimately, human supervision remains essential. Machines can assist, but humans must guide decisions with wisdom, ethics, and critical thinking.

Reflection

What does "narrow" mean in Artificial Narrow Intelligence?

Why can AI systems make mistakes?

How does bias affect AI decisions?

Why is it dangerous to rely too much on AI?

What role should humans play when using AI systems?

Worksheet

Part A: Vocabulary Matching

A. Bias
B. Data Dependence
C. Automation
D. Cybersecurity
E. Critical Thinking

___ Protecting systems from attacks

___ Relying on data to function

___ Unfair patterns in AI decisions

___ Machines performing tasks automatically

___ Evaluating and questioning information

Part B: Short Answer

What is one limitation of ANI?

Why does AI depend on data?

Give one example of bias in AI.

What is one risk of over-relying on AI?

Why is human supervision important?

Part C: Critical Thinking

Write a paragraph (5–7 sentences):

Explain why understanding the limits of AI is important for students and society.

Quiz (10 Questions)

What does ANI stand for?
A. Artificial Natural Intelligence
B. Artificial Narrow Intelligence
C. Automated Neural Integration
D. Advanced Network Intelligence

Why is ANI called "narrow"?
A. It is small
B. It performs one specific task
C. It is slow
D. It is simple

What is one limitation of ANI?
A. It can feel emotions
B. It can think like humans
C. It lacks true understanding
D. It works without data

Why is data important for AI?

A. It is optional
B. It helps machines learn patterns
C. It slows systems
D. It replaces machines

What is bias in AI?

A. Faster results
B. Accurate decisions
C. Unfair outcomes from data
D. Better learning

What is a risk of AI systems?

A. They are always correct
B. They cannot process data
C. Security vulnerabilities
D. They stop working

Why should humans use critical thinking with AI?

A. AI is perfect
B. AI can make mistakes
C. AI replaces thinking
D. AI is always wrong

How does AI impact jobs?

A. No impact
B. Only removes jobs
C. Changes job roles
D. Stops work

What is one environmental concern of AI?

A. Color
B. Speed

C. Energy consumption
D. Size

What is the main idea of the chapter?
A. AI has no limits
B. AI replaces humans
C. AI has limits and needs human guidance
D. AI is perfect

Answer Key

Worksheet Part A:

D

B

A

C

E

Quiz Answers:

B

B

C

B

C

C

B

C

C

C

CHAPTER 15 Preparing for the Next Level — From ANI to AGI

Introduction

Every generation stands at the edge of discovery — a threshold between what is known and what is yet to come.
For our generation, that threshold lies between **Artificial Narrow Intelligence (ANI)** and the emerging dream of **Artificial General Intelligence (AGI)**.

We have seen how ANI excels at specific tasks: translating languages, driving cars, diagnosing diseases, and composing music.
But these systems remain limited. They cannot think beyond their purpose or transfer knowledge from one field to another.
The next chapter in humanity's technological journey aims to overcome these limits — to create machines that can learn and reason *as broadly as humans do*.

This chapter prepares teachers and students to understand this transformation — not just as a technical shift, but as an *evolution of intelligence itself*.

From Specialization to Understanding

Artificial Narrow Intelligence can be compared to a student who memorizes answers but does not grasp concepts.
It performs brilliantly within a narrow field but struggles when the rules change.

Artificial General Intelligence, on the other hand, seeks to imitate the human ability to adapt.
It would not only solve problems but understand them — applying lessons from one experience to another.

Imagine a system that could diagnose a patient, write a summary report, learn a new language, and explain its reasoning — all without being reprogrammed.
That is the promise of AGI: *a machine that learns how to learn.*

Building Blocks of Transition

The journey from ANI to AGI begins with integrating the many narrow systems that exist today.
Each specialized program — whether for speech recognition, visual processing, or decision-

making — represents one fragment of intelligence.
Researchers now explore how to combine these fragments into a unified framework.

Several building blocks are essential for this transition:

- **Memory:** The ability to store knowledge from multiple domains and recall it when needed.
- **Reasoning:** The capacity to connect unrelated concepts and draw logical conclusions.
- **Adaptation:** Learning from new environments without explicit retraining.
- **Self-Reflection:** Understanding one's own actions and improving over time.

When these abilities merge, a system begins to resemble the flexible intelligence found in living beings.

The Human Brain as Inspiration

Scientists often look to the human brain for guidance in designing AGI.
The brain is a masterpiece of interconnected networks, constantly reorganizing itself through experience.
Each neuron learns not in isolation but in coordination with millions of others, forming patterns of thought and memory.

AI researchers try to replicate this through **neural networks** — mathematical structures inspired by biological neurons.
While today's ANI models can simulate small aspects of cognition, AGI will require something far more sophisticated: a digital mind capable of self-guided reasoning and understanding context like humans do.

Teachers can introduce this idea by comparing the brain to a living ecosystem — constantly growing, adapting, and learning from everything it encounters.

Learning Beyond Labels

One of the main challenges in moving beyond ANI is **unsupervised learning** — the ability to learn without being told exactly what to look for.
Most ANI systems rely on labeled data; they are trained by humans who tell them, "This is a cat," "This is a tree," "This is a sentence."

AGI will need to learn the way a child does — by exploring, experimenting, and discovering meaning through experience.
It will form its own understanding of the world, not by memorizing examples but by observing and reasoning.

This step transforms machines from reactive systems into proactive learners — capable of curiosity and creative problem-solving.

Humanity's Role in the Transition

The move from ANI to AGI is not just a technological evolution — it is a *human* one.
To create general intelligence responsibly, society must teach machines not only how to think, but how to act ethically.

Teachers and students hold a vital role in this transition:

- **Teachers** provide the moral framework — helping future developers understand fairness, compassion, and responsibility.
- **Students** bring imagination — the power to ask new questions and envision systems that serve the common good.

The classroom, therefore, becomes the birthplace of ethical intelligence — where knowledge meets conscience.

Challenges Ahead

Creating AGI poses enormous challenges.
Technically, researchers must build systems that can reason, imagine, and adapt in real time.
Ethically, humanity must decide what limits to set — how much autonomy to grant and how to ensure safety.

Philosophically, AGI raises questions that reach beyond science:
If a machine can think, what does it mean to be conscious?
If it learns faster than humans, how will we coexist?

These questions belong not only to engineers but to philosophers, artists, educators, and students — everyone who participates in the story of intelligence.

Preparing the Next Generation

Education must evolve alongside technology.
Students should be taught not only to *use* AI but to *understand* it — its logic, its limits, and its potential.
They must learn coding and critical thinking, but also empathy and ethics.

Schools can design interdisciplinary programs that blend science with social studies, philosophy with engineering, and creativity with computation.
Such education will produce balanced innovators — people who guide machines wisely rather than follow them blindly.

The Bridge Between Levels

Artificial Narrow Intelligence is the foundation upon which AGI will be built.
Every chatbot, translator, and autonomous system contributes a piece to the greater puzzle of

universal intelligence.
But before humanity builds minds that can reason like humans, it must first understand its own.

This bridge between ANI and AGI is not just technological — it is spiritual, intellectual, and ethical.
It asks humanity to define what intelligence truly means and to decide what kind of future it wants that intelligence to create.

Conclusion

The story of Artificial Narrow Intelligence is a story of specialization — of machines learning specific skills faster than humans ever could.
The story of Artificial General Intelligence will be one of unification — of connecting knowledge across boundaries, learning without limits, and reflecting human creativity and reason.

But every bridge must be built carefully.
As we move toward AGI, our greatest responsibility is not to make machines more human, but to make humanity more wise.

For teachers, this chapter represents the horizon of education — preparing young minds to live in an age of evolving intelligence.
For students, it marks the beginning of a new adventure — where understanding ANI is just the first step toward shaping the future of conscious technology.

CHAPTER 15 – TEACHER & STUDENT MATERIALS

(Preparing for the Next Level — From ANI to AGI)

Summary

Artificial Narrow Intelligence (ANI) is limited to specific tasks, but the future of AI aims to move toward Artificial General Intelligence (AGI), which would be able to think, learn, and adapt like humans.

AGI represents a shift from specialization to general understanding. Unlike ANI, AGI could apply knowledge across different areas and learn independently, similar to human learning.

To achieve this, systems must develop abilities such as memory, reasoning, adaptation, and self-reflection. Researchers often look to the human brain for inspiration, studying how it processes and connects information.

One major challenge is moving beyond labeled data toward unsupervised learning, where machines learn through exploration rather than instruction.

The transition to AGI is not only technical but also ethical. Humans must guide development responsibly, ensuring that future systems align with human values.

Education plays a key role in preparing students for this future by combining technical skills with ethical understanding.

Reflection

What is the difference between ANI and AGI?

Why is AGI considered more advanced than ANI?

What skills will future AI systems need to develop?

Why is human guidance important in developing AGI?

How can education prepare students for the future of AI?

Worksheet

Part A: Vocabulary Matching

A. AGI
B. ANI
C. Adaptation
D. Reasoning
E. Unsupervised Learning

___ Learning without labeled data

___ Ability to adjust to new situations

___ AI designed for specific tasks

___ AI that can think across multiple domains

___ Ability to connect ideas logically

Part B: Short Answer

What is Artificial General Intelligence (AGI)?

How is AGI different from ANI?

What is one building block needed for AGI?

Why is the human brain important in AI research?

What is unsupervised learning?

Part C: Critical Thinking

Write a paragraph (5–7 sentences):

Explain why the transition from ANI to AGI must be guided by ethics and responsibility.

Quiz (10 Questions)

What is AGI?
A. AI for one task
B. AI with general intelligence
C. A computer program
D. A robot tool

How is AGI different from ANI?
A. It is slower
B. It performs only one task
C. It can learn across multiple areas
D. It uses no data

What is one building block of AGI?
A. Size
B. Memory
C. Color
D. Speed

What does reasoning mean?
A. Guessing

B. Logical thinking
C. Memorizing
D. Ignoring data

What is adaptation?
A. Repeating tasks
B. Adjusting to new situations
C. Stopping learning
D. Avoiding change

What is unsupervised learning?
A. Learning with labels
B. Learning without guidance
C. No learning
D. Only human learning

Why do researchers study the human brain?
A. For fun
B. To design smarter AI systems
C. To replace humans
D. To stop AI

What role do humans play in AGI development?
A. No role
B. Guide ethics and design
C. Only provide data
D. Replace machines

What is a challenge of AGI?
A. It is easy to build
B. It requires no ethics
C. Technical and ethical complexity
D. It needs no learning

What is the main idea of the chapter?

A. AI will stop developing
B. AGI is impossible
C. AI is evolving toward general intelligence
D. AI should be ignored

Answer Key

Worksheet Part A:

E

C

B

A

D

Quiz Answers:

B

C

B

B

B

B

B

B

C

C

CHAPTER 16 How ANI Prepares Humanity for AGI — Lessons from the First Generation of Intelligent Machines

Introduction

Every generation passes a torch to the next.
For humanity, **Artificial Narrow Intelligence (ANI)** is that torch — a light guiding us toward a new frontier of learning, discovery, and responsibility.
While ANI represents the first stage of machine intelligence, it is also a classroom for humanity itself.

Through every smart assistant, search engine, medical scanner, and autonomous vehicle, ANI has taught people how machines think, how data behaves, and how algorithms mirror human decision-making.
This chapter explores how these experiences are preparing the world for **Artificial General Intelligence (AGI)** — a form of intelligence that could reason, learn, and adapt across many fields, just like the human mind.

Learning from Narrow Systems

The journey to AGI begins with lessons learned from narrow systems.
Each ANI application — whether in education, healthcare, or transportation — teaches humanity how machines interpret information and solve problems.

For instance:

- In education, AI tutoring tools reveal how learning patterns can be personalized.
- In healthcare, diagnostic systems demonstrate how machines analyze complex data to assist human judgment.
- In transportation, self-driving cars show how sensors and decision models cooperate to navigate the physical world.

Each example provides a different perspective on intelligence — from pattern recognition to decision-making — giving scientists and educators a foundation upon which to build the next level.

The Classroom of Humanity

Artificial Narrow Intelligence has become humanity's **classroom for digital literacy**.
Every interaction with technology — asking a voice assistant a question, using translation apps, or relying on GPS navigation — teaches users how intelligent systems operate.

Teachers can use these real-life tools to show students the principles of data, feedback, and learning loops.
In this sense, humanity itself has been enrolled in a global education program — learning how to coexist, collaborate, and communicate with machines.

Through ANI, society is not just developing smarter technology; it is training itself for a new kind of thinking — one that blends logic, ethics, and creativity.

Building the Ethical Foundation

Before humanity builds general intelligence, it must first build **ethical intelligence**.
ANI's early successes and mistakes have revealed the moral questions that come with intelligent systems:
How should data be collected?
Who is responsible when algorithms make errors?
How do we prevent bias and ensure fairness?

These experiences act as moral rehearsals for AGI.
By learning to design ANI systems with transparency and accountability, researchers are laying the foundation for more advanced intelligence that can be trusted.

Teachers can connect this to classroom ethics: just as students must learn honesty, fairness, and respect before earning independence, so must AI learn moral boundaries before gaining autonomy.

The Importance of Human Oversight

One of the greatest lessons ANI teaches is that intelligence without guidance can lead to imbalance.
Even the most advanced narrow systems still depend on **human supervision** — the wisdom that interprets data, corrects mistakes, and provides context.

For example:

- An AI program may detect fraud, but humans decide how to respond.
- A machine may recommend medical treatment, but doctors make the final decision.
- A chatbot may generate content, but educators ensure it aligns with truth and purpose.

Through these experiences, society is learning how to balance automation with responsibility.
This understanding will be critical as AGI emerges — ensuring that humans remain the moral compass behind intelligent technology.

Data as the Teacher

Every piece of data that ANI processes is a lesson in reality.
From photographs and sounds to words and numbers, data teaches machines how the world

works.
But it also teaches humanity how *we* work — how our habits, biases, and behaviors are reflected in technology.

By studying how ANI learns from data, researchers gain insights into human cognition.
This feedback loop — where humans teach machines and machines, in turn, teach humans — forms the core of progress toward AGI.

In schools, teachers can demonstrate this concept by comparing human learning (through experience and reflection) with machine learning (through data and feedback).
Both rely on the same universal principle: learning transforms through repetition, correction, and curiosity.

Imitation as the First Step to Understanding

In many ways, ANI's ability to mimic human actions represents the first step toward true understanding.
A child learns language by imitation before mastering meaning; similarly, AI systems learn by modeling human behavior before developing independent reasoning.

Voice assistants, translation models, and writing algorithms all operate through imitation — repeating patterns learned from data.
This imitation is not intelligence itself, but it builds the foundation upon which intelligence can grow.

AGI will likely emerge when imitation evolves into *abstraction* — when machines begin to understand why patterns exist, not just that they do.
Thus, ANI serves as the rehearsal stage for a more profound kind of intelligence yet to come.

Collaboration Between Humans and Machines

Every interaction between humans and ANI shapes the next generation of AI systems.
When doctors provide feedback to diagnostic models, or students correct an AI tutor, the machine learns.
At the same time, humans learn to communicate more precisely, think critically, and manage information more effectively.

This collaboration marks the birth of **co-evolutionary intelligence** — the process by which humans and machines grow together.
In this partnership, machines amplify human potential while humans guide machines with moral clarity.
This mutual growth is preparing the world for AGI — a form of intelligence that will not stand apart from humanity but evolve alongside it.

The Transition from Assistance to Autonomy

Artificial Narrow Intelligence assists; Artificial General Intelligence will adapt.
The transition between these stages will depend on how well humanity manages trust, control, and cooperation.

Already, ANI systems can act independently in limited contexts — piloting drones, managing warehouses, or optimizing energy grids.
But they still follow human-designed rules.
AGI will represent the point where machines can generate their own strategies, reasoning about entirely new situations.

The lessons humanity learns now — about safety, supervision, and ethics — will determine whether that autonomy strengthens or endangers society.

The Global Classroom

The rise of ANI has turned the entire planet into one vast learning environment.
Children in Fiji can use translation apps to connect with classrooms in Japan.
Students in the U.S. can collaborate with AI-driven tutors that adapt to their unique learning styles.
Farmers, engineers, artists, and scientists all share knowledge through intelligent tools.

This collective education prepares humanity for a future where intelligence — both human and artificial — becomes a shared global resource.
By learning together, nations can ensure that AGI emerges not as a private invention, but as a collective achievement.

Conclusion

Artificial Narrow Intelligence is humanity's training ground — the first great experiment in teaching machines to learn.
Through ANI, humans are discovering what intelligence means, how it behaves, and how it must be guided.

The lessons are profound:

- That technology reflects our values.
- That intelligence requires ethics.
- That collaboration creates progress.

By mastering these lessons now, teachers and students help build a bridge of understanding that will carry the world safely into the age of AGI.

ANI is not the end of the story — it is the beginning of a greater one.
It is humanity's first teacher in the language of artificial thought — and the foundation upon which the next generation of intelligent life will rise.

CHAPTER 16 – TEACHER & STUDENT MATERIALS

Learning from Artificial Narrow Intelligence — The Foundation for the Future of AI

Extended Summary

Artificial Narrow Intelligence (ANI) represents the current stage of artificial intelligence, where machines are designed to perform specific tasks with high accuracy. This chapter explores how ANI is not just a technological tool, but a critical learning phase for humanity as it prepares for more advanced forms of intelligence, such as Artificial General Intelligence (AGI).

ANI systems are already deeply integrated into everyday life. From voice assistants and recommendation systems to medical diagnostics and navigation tools, these systems demonstrate how machines can process information, recognize patterns, and assist humans in solving complex problems. However, despite their impressive capabilities, ANI systems remain limited to the tasks they were designed to perform.

This limitation is what makes ANI such an important learning opportunity. By interacting with ANI, humans gain a deeper understanding of how intelligence can be modeled, how data influences decisions, and how systems can be improved over time. In many ways, ANI serves as a "training ground" — not just for machines, but for people.

The chapter emphasizes that ANI teaches important lessons about both technology and responsibility. It reveals how data quality affects outcomes, how bias can influence results, and how human oversight is essential to ensure accuracy and fairness. These lessons are critical as society moves toward more advanced AI systems.

Another key idea is that ANI helps build digital literacy. Students and educators learn how to use, evaluate, and question AI systems. This understanding empowers individuals to interact with technology more effectively and responsibly.

The chapter also highlights that ANI is shaping industries and creating new opportunities. While some tasks are automated, new roles are emerging that require a combination of technical skills and human insight. This shift encourages students to develop adaptability, problem-solving abilities, and lifelong learning habits.

Ultimately, ANI is not the final destination of artificial intelligence — it is the foundation. It prepares humanity for the next phase by providing knowledge, experience, and awareness. The better humans understand ANI, the better prepared they will be to guide future advancements in AI.

In conclusion, ANI is more than just a collection of tools; it is a learning experience for society. It teaches humans how to think about intelligence, how to design responsible systems, and how to prepare for a future where technology plays an even greater role. The lessons learned from ANI today will shape the intelligent systems of tomorrow.

Reflection

What is Artificial Narrow Intelligence (ANI)?

How is ANI used in everyday life?

Why is ANI considered a "learning phase" for humanity?

What are the limitations of ANI?

How does ANI help build digital literacy?

What lessons can humans learn from AI systems?

Why is human oversight important when using AI?

How is ANI changing industries and jobs?

What skills should students develop because of AI?

How does ANI prepare society for the future of AI?

Worksheet

Part A: Vocabulary Matching

A. Artificial Narrow Intelligence
B. Digital Literacy
C. Algorithm
D. Automation
E. Data

___ Information used to train AI systems

___ Step-by-step instructions for solving a problem

___ AI designed to perform specific tasks

___ Machines performing tasks automatically

___ Understanding and using technology effectively

Part B: Short Answer

Give one example of ANI in real life.

What is one limitation of ANI?

Why is data important in AI systems?

What does digital literacy mean?

How does ANI help prepare for future AI developments?

Part C: Critical Thinking

Write a paragraph (5–7 sentences):

Explain why learning about ANI is important for students today. Include both benefits and responsibilities.

Quiz (10 Questions)

What does ANI stand for?
A. Artificial Natural Intelligence
B. Artificial Narrow Intelligence
C. Automated Neural Integration
D. Advanced Network Intelligence

What is the main idea of this chapter?
A. AI replaces humans
B. ANI is the foundation for future AI
C. Technology is not important
D. AI is complete

What is one example of ANI?
A. Human brain
B. Voice assistant
C. Teacher
D. Student

What is a limitation of ANI?

A. It can think like humans
B. It can perform any task
C. It is limited to specific tasks
D. It has emotions

Why is data important in AI?

A. It slows systems
B. It helps AI learn patterns
C. It is not needed
D. It replaces humans

What is digital literacy?

A. Ignoring technology
B. Understanding and using technology
C. Avoiding machines
D. Playing games

What does automation mean?

A. Manual work
B. Machines performing tasks
C. Stopping systems
D. Human-only work

Why is human oversight important?

A. AI is perfect
B. AI can make mistakes
C. AI replaces humans
D. AI does not need help

How is ANI affecting jobs?

A. No change
B. Only removing jobs
C. Changing job roles
D. Stopping work

What is the key message of the chapter?

A. ANI is the final stage of AI
B. ANI helps prepare humans for future AI
C. AI is not useful
D. Technology should stop

Answer Key

Worksheet Part A:

E

C

A

D

B

Quiz Answers:

B

B

B

C

B

B

B

B

C

B

CHAPTER 17 The Global Impact of ANI — How the First Intelligent Systems Are Reshaping Civilization

Introduction

Every new age of invention changes how people live and think.
The steam engine began the Industrial Revolution; electricity powered the modern world; and now **Artificial Narrow Intelligence (ANI)** is redefining the twenty-first century.

ANI is not confined to laboratories or apps — it is embedded in hospitals, farms, schools, transportation systems, and governments.
It influences how food is grown, how energy is distributed, how students learn, and how nations communicate.
This chapter explores how the first intelligent systems are transforming civilization — connecting humanity across cultures while challenging society to use this power wisely.

A World Connected by Intelligence

The most visible global effect of ANI is connectivity.
Through intelligent translation tools, voice assistants, and global information networks, people can now communicate across languages and continents instantly.

A teacher in Fiji can share lessons with classrooms in Canada.
A doctor in India can consult data analyzed by a system in Germany.
Farmers in Africa can use satellite-driven ANI tools to predict rainfall and prevent crop loss.

These connections form a **global web of knowledge** — a living network where information flows freely, linking human insight with machine precision.
For the first time in history, intelligence is no longer limited by geography.

Transforming the Global Economy

The rise of ANI has reshaped economies worldwide.
Industries once dependent on manual labor now rely on intelligent automation.
Factories use AI-driven robots to assemble products with speed and accuracy.
Financial institutions analyze global markets in seconds.
Small entrepreneurs use recommendation algorithms to reach international customers.

While this transformation creates new opportunities for growth, it also introduces new inequalities.
Countries with stronger access to digital infrastructure advance rapidly, while others risk being left behind.

Teachers can guide classroom discussions about this "intelligence divide," helping students explore how fair access to technology can empower rather than divide humanity.

A balanced economy requires global cooperation — ensuring that innovation benefits everyone, not just a few.

Education Without Borders

Education has perhaps changed more than any other field.
Artificial Narrow Intelligence has turned classrooms into global learning environments.
Intelligent tutoring systems adjust lessons to each student's pace.
Translation engines allow students to study materials in any language.
AI-powered research tools help teachers design personalized activities.

In remote regions, virtual classrooms supported by ANI bring quality education to places once out of reach.
Through these advances, learning becomes universal — not limited by wealth or geography.

Yet this progress carries a challenge: technology should *enhance* teaching, not *replace* teachers.
True education still requires human mentorship, empathy, and encouragement.

Healthcare and Human Well-Being

In medicine, ANI is saving lives.
Diagnostic algorithms detect diseases from X-rays or genetic data faster than human experts.
Predictive models identify outbreaks before they spread.
Wearable devices monitor vital signs, warning patients of health risks in real time.

These tools make healthcare more efficient and accessible, especially in developing nations where medical resources are limited.
However, they also raise ethical questions: How should personal health data be stored? Who decides which treatments AI recommends?

By discussing these issues in classrooms, teachers help students connect technology with compassion — reminding them that healthcare must always serve people, not profit.

Agriculture and Food Security

Feeding the world's growing population is one of humanity's greatest challenges.
ANI plays a crucial role in this mission.
Intelligent sensors analyze soil quality, temperature, and moisture to optimize planting.
Drones equipped with AI identify diseased crops early, reducing waste and improving yields.

Farmers, even in small villages, can access cloud-based ANI platforms that forecast weather or recommend fertilizers.
This global network of "smart farming" has begun to reduce hunger and stabilize food systems.

In this way, ANI reconnects technology to nature — teaching students that intelligence can also mean understanding the earth.

Environmental and Energy Solutions

Climate change is a global crisis that demands intelligent solutions.
ANI is being used to track deforestation, monitor air pollution, and predict extreme weather events.
Energy grids powered by AI balance electricity supply and demand, preventing waste and reducing carbon emissions.

Scientists are training algorithms to model ocean temperatures, protect endangered species, and design renewable energy systems.
Through these innovations, ANI becomes not just a tool of industry but a **guardian of the planet**.

This aligns perfectly with classroom values of sustainability — teaching students that intelligence must protect the Earth that sustains it.

Cultural Exchange and Creative Collaboration

ANI is transforming art, language, and culture on a global scale.
Artists use intelligent systems to collaborate across continents — combining different styles, traditions, and rhythms into new forms of expression.
Writers and musicians partner with AI tools to experiment with storytelling and sound.

Translation models make literature from every language accessible to readers worldwide.
Cultural heritage projects use ANI to restore damaged paintings and digitize ancient manuscripts.

These advances celebrate humanity's diversity — proving that creativity expands when cultures and technologies meet.

Government, Justice, and Public Service

Governments worldwide are turning to ANI to improve public systems.
Traffic optimization algorithms reduce congestion in major cities.
AI-driven analytics help allocate resources for schools, hospitals, and emergency response.
Predictive models monitor environmental hazards and prevent disasters.

However, these systems must be designed with fairness and transparency.
When algorithms influence justice or public policy, citizens must understand how decisions are made.
Teaching civic awareness in this context prepares students to be thoughtful digital citizens — equipped to question, evaluate, and shape the intelligent systems that govern their world.

Global Challenges and Shared Responsibility

With great power comes global responsibility.
The rise of ANI introduces new ethical, social, and political questions that transcend national borders:
Who owns the data that drives global systems?
How can nations ensure security while promoting openness?
What happens when intelligent automation displaces workers faster than economies can adapt?

These questions cannot be answered by one country alone.
They require international cooperation — educators, scientists, and leaders working together to define principles of fairness, accountability, and sustainability.

Teachers can inspire students to think globally: to see themselves as part of a shared mission — building intelligence that serves humanity as a whole.

A Civilization in Transition

Humanity is now in a transitional era — moving from industrial society to intelligent civilization.
Just as the Industrial Revolution reshaped cities and labor, the Intelligence Revolution is reshaping communication, creativity, and consciousness.

ANI has become the invisible architecture of modern life.
It connects nations, automates industries, enhances medicine, and preserves culture.
But its true impact lies in what it reveals about humanity: that intelligence, whether human or artificial, thrives only when guided by purpose and compassion.

Conclusion

The global impact of Artificial Narrow Intelligence is nothing less than a new chapter in civilization's story.
It is connecting people who were once divided, amplifying knowledge, and offering solutions to challenges once thought unsolvable.
Yet it also reminds the world that technology alone cannot create justice, peace, or wisdom — those remain human responsibilities.

For teachers, this chapter is a guide to global citizenship in the age of intelligence.
For students, it is a call to action — to learn, question, and build a future where intelligence uplifts rather than divides.

ANI has already changed the world.
What humanity chooses to do next will determine whether it becomes the foundation of harmony — or the first test of our collective wisdom.

CHAPTER 17 – TEACHER & STUDENT MATERIALS

Human and AI Collaboration — Working Together in an Intelligent World

Extended Summary

As artificial intelligence becomes more integrated into daily life, the relationship between humans and machines is evolving from simple use to meaningful collaboration. This chapter explores how humans and AI can work together to achieve better outcomes than either could alone.

Artificial Intelligence is exceptionally strong at processing large amounts of data, recognizing patterns, and performing repetitive tasks with speed and accuracy. However, it lacks qualities that define human intelligence, such as creativity, emotional understanding, ethical reasoning, and the ability to interpret complex social situations.

Humans, on the other hand, bring judgment, empathy, imagination, and moral responsibility. These uniquely human qualities allow people to make decisions that consider context, values, and long-term consequences. When combined with the computational power of AI, this creates a powerful partnership.

The chapter emphasizes that AI should not be viewed as a replacement for humans, but as a tool that enhances human capability. In fields such as healthcare, AI can analyze medical data quickly, while doctors make final decisions based on experience and compassion. In education, AI can support personalized learning, while teachers guide, inspire, and mentor students.

This collaboration requires understanding and balance. Humans must learn how AI works in order to use it effectively, while also recognizing its limitations. Over-reliance on AI without critical thinking can lead to errors, while underuse can limit opportunities for improvement.

Another key idea is shared responsibility. Humans remain accountable for decisions made with the help of AI. This means that users, developers, and organizations must ensure that AI systems are used ethically and responsibly.

Students are encouraged to see themselves as future collaborators with AI. Rather than competing with machines, they should develop skills that complement AI — such as creativity, communication, leadership, and ethical thinking.

In conclusion, the future is not about humans versus machines, but humans working with machines. This partnership has the potential to solve complex problems, improve lives, and create new opportunities. However, it must always be guided by human values, responsibility, and wisdom.

Reflection

How do humans and AI work together in real life?

What strengths does AI have compared to humans?

What strengths do humans have that AI cannot replace?

Why is it important to see AI as a partner rather than a replacement?

What risks exist if humans rely too much on AI?

How can collaboration improve outcomes in fields like healthcare or education?

Why is human judgment important when using AI?

What skills should students develop to work effectively with AI?

Who is responsible for decisions made using AI?

How can you personally use AI responsibly in your daily life?

Worksheet

Part A: Vocabulary Matching

A. Collaboration
B. Artificial Intelligence
C. Ethics
D. Creativity
E. Data Processing

___ Working together toward a shared goal

___ Technology that simulates human intelligence

___ Human ability to imagine and create new ideas

___ Handling and analyzing large amounts of information

___ Moral principles guiding decisions

Part B: Short Answer

What is one strength of AI?

What is one strength of humans?

Why is collaboration between humans and AI important?

How does AI help in healthcare or education?

Why must humans remain responsible when using AI?

Part C: Critical Thinking

Write a paragraph (5–7 sentences):

Explain why humans and AI should work together instead of competing. Include examples of strengths from both.

Quiz (10 Questions)

What is the main idea of this chapter?
A. AI replaces humans
B. Humans and AI should collaborate
C. AI should be avoided
D. Humans cannot use AI

What is one strength of AI?
A. Emotional understanding
B. Creativity
C. Processing large amounts of data
D. Moral reasoning

What is one strength of humans?
A. Fast calculations
B. Emotional understanding and judgment
C. Data storage
D. Automation

Why should AI be seen as a partner?
A. It replaces humans
B. It works best with human guidance
C. It removes jobs
D. It stops thinking

What is collaboration?
A. Working alone
B. Competing

C. Working together
D. Avoiding tasks

What is a risk of over-relying on AI?
A. Faster results
B. Perfect decisions
C. Errors without human review
D. Better learning

Who is responsible for AI decisions?
A. Machines
B. Humans
C. Robots
D. No one

How can AI help in education?
A. Replace teachers
B. Personalize learning
C. Stop learning
D. Remove students

What skill is important for working with AI?
A. Ignoring technology
B. Creativity and critical thinking
C. Avoiding learning
D. Memorizing only

What is the key message of the chapter?
A. AI is dangerous
B. Humans and AI must work together responsibly
C. AI replaces all jobs
D. Technology is not needed

Answer Key

Worksheet Part A:

A

B

D

E

C

Quiz Answers:

B

C

B

B

C

C

B

B

B

B

CHAPTER 18 The Future of Learning in the Age of ANI — Schools, Students, and Smart Systems

Introduction

Education is the heartbeat of every civilization.
It is how knowledge is passed, dreams are nurtured, and societies evolve.
Today, in the age of **Artificial Narrow Intelligence (ANI)**, education is experiencing its most profound transformation since the invention of the printing press.

Classrooms are no longer confined by walls or time zones.
Students can learn at their own pace, explore any subject instantly, and connect with mentors across the world.
Teachers are becoming designers of experiences — guiding students through personalized journeys shaped by intelligent tools.

This chapter explores how ANI is reshaping learning — what it means for schools, teachers, and students — and how humanity can use this technology to create a more just, creative, and inclusive future for all learners.

The Evolution of the Classroom

For centuries, learning followed a single model: a teacher in front of a classroom, students listening, reading, and writing on paper.
While this structure built strong foundations, it often limited creativity and individual growth.

With the arrival of Artificial Narrow Intelligence, classrooms are evolving into **dynamic ecosystems of learning**.
Lessons are no longer static; they are interactive, adaptive, and personalized.
Students receive feedback instantly, and teachers can see each learner's progress in real time.

In this new environment, learning becomes less about memorizing facts and more about developing curiosity, problem-solving, and understanding.

Personalized Learning Paths

Every student learns differently — some visually, others through listening, reading, or doing.
ANI recognizes these differences and creates customized learning experiences.

By analyzing data such as quiz results, reading patterns, and engagement levels, AI-powered systems adjust lessons to meet each student's needs.
For example, if a student struggles with fractions, the system offers more visual examples; if another student excels in writing, it presents advanced composition tasks.

This personalization ensures that no student is left behind and no mind is left unstimulated.
It gives each learner ownership of their education — turning classrooms into laboratories of personal growth.

Teachers as Guides of Intelligence

In the age of ANI, the role of the teacher becomes more vital than ever.
Technology can deliver information, but it cannot inspire purpose, empathy, or wisdom.
Teachers are now **mentors, facilitators, and ethical guides**, helping students interpret what machines cannot explain.

With intelligent analytics, teachers can focus less on grading and more on mentoring.
They can identify emotional or cognitive challenges early and provide human support where machines cannot.
This partnership between teacher and technology forms a new model of education — one built on empathy supported by intelligence.

Smart Classrooms and Virtual Learning

Schools around the world are integrating ANI into their physical and virtual spaces.
Smartboards respond to voice commands, digital assistants schedule assignments, and interactive textbooks adapt to student progress.

Virtual classrooms powered by ANI connect students from multiple countries, allowing real-time collaboration on projects.
A science class in California can share data with a class in Tonga; a math class in Japan can co-solve equations with peers in Kenya.

These experiences cultivate **global learning communities**, where technology bridges cultures and promotes understanding across borders.

Assessment and Feedback in Real Time

Traditional assessments — exams, essays, and report cards — often reflect what a student knew weeks or months ago.
ANI changes that by offering **continuous evaluation**.

Intelligent platforms track learning as it happens, providing instant feedback to both teachers and students.
Students can see their strengths and weaknesses immediately, while teachers can adjust lessons before frustration or confusion sets in.

This real-time feedback encourages growth, not judgment.
It transforms education from a series of tests into a process of discovery and improvement.

Accessibility and Inclusion

One of ANI's greatest contributions to education is inclusion.
Students with disabilities can now access tools that support speech recognition, reading assistance, translation, and visual guidance.
Language barriers dissolve through automatic interpretation.
Remote learners can attend school from home or rural areas where teachers are scarce.

Intelligent systems also adapt content for emotional and social learning, helping students with autism or learning differences engage confidently.

For the first time, education is moving toward **true equality of opportunity** — where every learner has access to the resources they need to thrive.

Ethical Education for the Digital Generation

As students grow up surrounded by intelligent systems, they must learn to use them responsibly. Ethics and digital citizenship are now as essential as reading and mathematics.

Classrooms must teach not only how AI works but how it should be used.
Students should learn about privacy, bias, transparency, and the social impact of data-driven systems.
They should also understand that intelligence is not only measured by logic — but also by compassion and moral reasoning.

In this sense, the future of learning is not just about teaching machines — it's about teaching humanity to think wisely in a digital world.

The Teacher–Machine Partnership

Education's new partnership is not humans versus machines, but humans *with* machines.
ANI handles data analysis, grading, and organization.
Teachers bring context, connection, and care.
Together, they form a **hybrid model of intelligence** that strengthens both.

Students benefit from the best of both worlds — the precision of technology and the warmth of mentorship.
This partnership demonstrates the heart of ethical AI: intelligence guided by empathy.

Global Knowledge Networks

The world is now one vast learning network.
Online libraries, research databases, and open-access platforms provide students with more knowledge than any single school could contain.
ANI curates this information, recommending trustworthy sources and filtering misinformation.

Through shared global projects — from climate research to cultural studies — students learn that intelligence grows through cooperation, not competition.
They begin to see themselves not only as learners but as contributors to a global mission of understanding.

Challenges of AI in Education

Despite its benefits, ANI also brings challenges.
Schools must ensure data privacy and fairness in automated systems.
Teachers need training to use AI effectively and ethically.
Societies must ensure that no community is excluded from digital access.

These challenges remind us that progress requires balance — innovation guided by humanity's moral compass.
In addressing them, educators and students become guardians of the next educational revolution.

The Future School

The school of the future will not be defined by walls, but by connection.
Learning will happen everywhere — in classrooms, homes, communities, and virtual spaces — guided by intelligent systems that know each learner's rhythm.

Students will explore subjects that combine science, art, and ethics.
Teachers will mentor global classrooms of thinkers and creators.
Technology will fade into the background, allowing curiosity to lead the way.

Education will become a lifelong journey — personalized, ethical, and connected.

Conclusion

Artificial Narrow Intelligence is reshaping the very meaning of education.
It transforms learning into a living process — adaptive, inclusive, and global.
But its greatest achievement is not in automation or data; it is in the opportunity it gives humanity to redefine *how* and *why* we learn.

For teachers, this chapter represents the dawn of a new era of teaching — one guided by wisdom, compassion, and technology.
For students, it is a promise that their classrooms are becoming laboratories of the future — where imagination meets intelligence.

When guided by care and curiosity, ANI does more than teach — it awakens the learner within every human being.
The future of learning belongs to those who see technology not as competition, but as a partner in the pursuit of wisdom.

CHAPTER 18 – TEACHER & STUDENT MATERIALS

Education in the Age of Artificial Intelligence — Preparing for a Changing World

Extended Summary

As artificial intelligence continues to transform industries and daily life, education must evolve to prepare students for a future shaped by intelligent systems. This chapter explores how schools, teachers, and students must adapt to meet the demands of an AI-driven world.

Traditionally, education focused on memorization and repetition. However, in a world where AI can quickly access and process information, the value of learning has shifted. Students must now focus on understanding concepts, solving problems, thinking critically, and applying knowledge in meaningful ways.

Artificial Intelligence is already being used in classrooms to personalize learning, assist teachers, and provide real-time feedback. These tools can help identify student strengths and weaknesses, allowing for more individualized instruction. However, while AI can support education, it cannot replace the human elements of teaching — such as encouragement, empathy, mentorship, and inspiration.

The chapter emphasizes the importance of developing both technical and human-centered skills. Students must become digitally literate, understanding how AI works and how to use it responsibly. At the same time, they must strengthen skills that machines cannot replicate easily — including creativity, communication, collaboration, and ethical decision-making.

Another key concept introduced is lifelong learning. In a rapidly changing technological environment, learning does not end after school. Students must be prepared to continuously adapt, update their skills, and embrace new knowledge throughout their lives.

Teachers also play a critical role in this transformation. They are not only instructors but guides who help students navigate technology responsibly. By integrating AI into lessons thoughtfully, teachers can prepare students to become informed and capable participants in a digital society.

This chapter encourages schools to move toward interdisciplinary learning — combining science, technology, ethics, and the humanities. Such an approach ensures that students are not only technically skilled but also socially and ethically aware.

In conclusion, education is the foundation of the AI future. The goal is not to compete with machines, but to develop human strengths that complement them. By preparing students with knowledge, adaptability, and responsibility, schools can ensure that the next generation is ready to thrive in an AI-powered world.

Reflection

How is education changing because of AI?

Why is memorization less important in today's world?

What are some skills that AI cannot replace?

What is digital literacy, and why is it important?

Why is lifelong learning necessary in an AI-driven world?

How can AI support teachers and students?

Why are human skills like creativity and empathy still important?

What role do teachers play in preparing students for AI?

How can schools adapt to new technology?

How can you prepare yourself for the future of AI?

Worksheet

Part A: Vocabulary Matching

A. Digital Literacy
B. Lifelong Learning
C. Artificial Intelligence
D. Critical Thinking
E. Collaboration

___ Working together with others

___ Understanding and using technology effectively

___ Continuous learning throughout life

___ Technology that simulates human intelligence

___ Analyzing and evaluating information

Part B: Short Answer

What is one way AI is used in education today?

Why is memorization no longer enough?

Name one human skill that AI cannot replace.

What is lifelong learning?

Why is digital literacy important for students?

Part C: Critical Thinking

Write a paragraph (5–7 sentences):

Explain how education must change to prepare students for an AI-driven future. Include both technical and human skills.

Quiz (10 Questions)

What is the main focus of this chapter?
A. Replacing teachers with AI
B. Preparing education for an AI-driven future
C. Removing technology from schools
D. Memorizing information

Why is memorization less important today?
A. It is easier
B. AI can store and access information quickly
C. It is not needed at all
D. It slows learning

What is digital literacy?
A. Reading books
B. Understanding and using technology
C. Avoiding computers
D. Writing essays

What is lifelong learning?
A. Learning only in school
B. Continuous learning throughout life
C. No learning
D. Short-term learning

What is one skill AI cannot easily replace?
A. Data storage
B. Creativity
C. Speed
D. Calculation

How can AI help in education?
A. Replace teachers completely
B. Personalize learning
C. Stop learning
D. Remove students

What role do teachers play in AI education?
A. No role
B. Guide and mentor students
C. Replace machines
D. Avoid technology

What is critical thinking?
A. Memorizing facts
B. Evaluating and analyzing information
C. Ignoring information
D. Avoiding decisions

Why is collaboration important?
A. It slows work
B. It helps people work together effectively
C. It removes ideas
D. It avoids learning

What is the key message of this chapter?
A. AI will replace education
B. Education must evolve to prepare students for AI
C. Technology is not important
D. Learning should stop

Answer Key

Worksheet Part A:

E

A

B

C

D

Quiz Answers:

B

B

B

B

B

B

B

B

B

B

CHAPTER 19 The Human Values Behind ANI — Compassion, Creativity, and Conscious Learning

Introduction

Artificial Narrow Intelligence (ANI) has shown the world how machines can think, analyze, and predict.
But beyond the circuits, algorithms, and data lies a greater question — *what kind of intelligence do we want to create?*

Humanity's greatest strength has never been speed or precision; it has been heart.
The ability to feel compassion, imagine the impossible, and act with moral awareness is what distinguishes human intelligence from artificial intelligence.

This chapter reminds students and teachers that technology should not only make us smarter — it should make us more *human*.
ANI becomes meaningful only when guided by empathy, creativity, and conscious understanding.

Compassion — The Heart of True Intelligence

Compassion is the ability to understand and care for the feelings of others.
It is what turns knowledge into kindness and intelligence into wisdom.

Machines can analyze emotions through tone or facial expressions, but they cannot truly feel them.
That responsibility belongs to people.
When humans use ANI to help others — predicting natural disasters, detecting diseases early, or assisting the elderly — compassion becomes the moral engine behind innovation. For example, AI is used to detect early signs of disease, allowing doctors to treat patients sooner and save lives.

Teachers can help students explore this by asking:
"How can technology heal rather than harm? How can it unite rather than divide?"

The answer lies not in programming alone, but in the *intentions* of those who design and use it.

Creativity — The Spirit of Human Expression

Creativity is the force that gives birth to every invention, story, and discovery.
It is the spark that transforms information into imagination.

ANI can generate music, write stories, and design art — but it does so by rearranging existing patterns.
Human creativity, by contrast, arises from emotion, experience, and the desire to express meaning.

When a poet writes, a scientist experiments, or a child draws, they are not following data — they are expressing their inner world.
ANI can assist in this process — providing inspiration, exploring color, rhythm, or composition — but it cannot dream.

The true partnership between human and machine happens when creativity meets computation: when the artist uses technology as a canvas, and the machine becomes a mirror reflecting human possibility.

Conscious Learning — Awareness in the Age of Intelligence

Conscious learning is more than memorization or repetition; it is the practice of awareness.
It asks, *Why am I learning this? How can this knowledge make the world better?*

In the age of ANI, learning risks becoming mechanical — collecting information without reflection.
To balance this, schools must teach students how to think critically, ask questions, and connect knowledge with purpose.

Conscious learning means recognizing that every algorithm and dataset carries human fingerprints — our values, our biases, and our hopes.
By understanding this, students become conscious creators of technology rather than passive users.

Ethical Imagination — Thinking with the Heart and the Mind

Ethical imagination is the ability to foresee the consequences of our creations and to guide innovation with empathy.
Before designing an intelligent system, developers must imagine how it could affect lives — positively or negatively.

When scientists imagine an AI that helps farmers grow food or doctors save lives, they use ethical imagination.
When engineers build systems that respect privacy and fairness, they combine logic with conscience.

Teachers can nurture this quality through storytelling, debate, and creative design projects that ask:
"What problem does this technology solve, and who does it serve?"
Such exercises remind students that the best innovations are those that uplift humanity.

Cultural Intelligence and Respect for Diversity

Human intelligence is shaped by culture, language, and tradition.
ANI, trained on global data, must learn to respect that diversity.
If not guided carefully, it can unintentionally favor one worldview or silence another.

Cultural intelligence means teaching machines — and students — to recognize and value different perspectives.
When developers include diverse data sources, languages, and histories, technology becomes more inclusive.

In classrooms, students can learn from this principle by studying how AI tools interpret languages, art, or customs from around the world.
They will discover that intelligence, in its highest form, celebrates *diversity as wisdom.*

The Role of Teachers in Humanizing Technology

Teachers are the guardians of humanity in the digital age.
Their mission is not only to teach science and mathematics but to preserve compassion, curiosity, and moral vision.

In a world shaped by ANI, teachers guide students to see technology not as a replacement for human connection, but as a pathway to deeper understanding.
They help learners balance innovation with empathy — showing that progress without heart is incomplete.

By teaching ethical reflection, emotional intelligence, and global awareness, educators ensure that future generations will use ANI to build bridges, not barriers.

The Emotional Dimension of Learning

Every student brings emotions into the learning process — joy, curiosity, frustration, hope.
ANI systems can measure engagement, but they cannot comfort, encourage, or celebrate success.
Only a teacher's smile, a friend's support, or a parent's pride can transform learning into growth.

Understanding this emotional dimension keeps education grounded in humanity.
It reminds students that while machines can teach information, only people can teach inspiration.

The Balance Between Logic and Love

Logic guides technology; love gives it purpose.
A balanced civilization requires both — reason to build systems, and compassion to guide them.

As machines become smarter, humanity must become wiser.
That wisdom begins when people choose kindness as the foundation of progress.
Every line of code, every algorithm, every innovation should ask: *Does this help someone? Does it bring more understanding into the world?*

When logic and love work together, intelligence becomes a force for harmony.

The Global Classroom of Humanity

The rise of ANI has turned the entire planet into a shared classroom.
Students in one part of the world can collaborate with peers thousands of miles away.
Together, they learn not only science and technology but empathy and cooperation.

This global classroom teaches that intelligence is not a competition of machines — it is a collaboration of minds.
Human values like compassion, respect, and curiosity are the universal languages that unite this new civilization of learning.

Conclusion

Artificial Narrow Intelligence reflects what humanity teaches it — our strengths, our dreams, and our flaws.
If we want machines to act wisely, we must lead them with heart.
Compassion, creativity, and conscious learning are not separate from technology; they are the foundation upon which true intelligence stands.

For teachers, this chapter is a reminder that education is not just about preparing students for jobs — it is about preparing them for life in a world shared with intelligent systems.
For students, it is an invitation to lead with empathy and imagination — to become the generation that humanizes technology.

When intelligence and compassion walk hand in hand, machines become mirrors of our highest selves.
And in that reflection, humanity discovers not the future of AI — but the future of itself.

CHAPTER 19 – TEACHER & STUDENT MATERIALS

Ethics, Responsibility, and Trust in Artificial Intelligence

Extended Summary

As artificial intelligence becomes more powerful and widely used, the question is no longer just *what AI can do*, but *what AI should do*. This chapter explores the critical role of ethics, responsibility, and trust in the development and use of AI systems.

Artificial Intelligence is built by humans, trained on human data, and used in human society. Because of this, AI systems often reflect both the strengths and weaknesses of the people who create them. If not carefully designed, AI can produce unfair outcomes, reinforce bias, or make decisions that negatively impact individuals and communities.

Ethics in AI refers to the principles that guide how technology should be used responsibly. These include fairness, transparency, accountability, and respect for human rights. For example, an AI system used in hiring must treat all candidates equally, while a healthcare AI must prioritize patient safety and accuracy.

The chapter also introduces the concept of responsibility. When an AI system makes a mistake, who is accountable? Is it the developer, the company, or the user? These questions highlight the importance of human oversight. AI cannot take responsibility for its actions — only humans can.

Trust is another essential element. People must feel confident that AI systems are safe, reliable, and fair. Trust is built through transparency (understanding how AI works), consistent performance, and ethical design. Without trust, even the most advanced technologies will not be accepted or used effectively.

Students are encouraged to think critically about how AI is used in society and to recognize their future role in shaping ethical technology. They are not just users of AI but future designers, decision-makers, and leaders who will influence how AI impacts the world.

In conclusion, the development of AI must always be guided by human values. Technology alone cannot ensure fairness or justice — it requires thoughtful, responsible people. As AI continues to grow, the need for ethical awareness becomes even more important. The future of AI depends not just on innovation, but on integrity.

Reflection

What does ethics mean in the context of AI?

Why is fairness important when designing AI systems?

Who should be responsible when AI makes a mistake?

Why is trust important in using AI technologies?

How can bias affect AI decisions?

What does transparency mean in AI systems?

Why can AI not make ethical decisions on its own?

How can students help create responsible AI in the future?

What risks exist if AI is not guided by ethics?

How can society build trust in AI systems?

Worksheet

Part A: Vocabulary Matching

A. Ethics
B. Bias
C. Transparency
D. Accountability
E. Trust

___ Being responsible for actions and decisions

___ Openness about how systems work

___ Confidence in reliability and fairness

___ Unfair patterns in data or decisions

___ Moral principles guiding behavior

Part B: Short Answer

What is ethical AI?

Why is bias a problem in AI systems?

What does accountability mean in AI?

Why is transparency important?

How can humans ensure AI is used responsibly?

Part C: Critical Thinking

Write a paragraph (5–7 sentences):

Explain why ethics is essential in the development and use of AI. Include examples of fairness, responsibility, and trustQuiz (10 Questions)

What is ethics in AI?
A. Speed of machines
B. Rules for building computers
C. Moral principles guiding AI use
D. Programming language

Why is fairness important in AI?
A. To make systems faster
B. To ensure equal treatment
C. To reduce costs
D. To simplify coding

What is bias in AI?
A. Accurate data
B. Neutral decisions
C. Unfair patterns in data
D. Faster processing

What does transparency mean?
A. Hiding information
B. Showing how AI works
C. Speeding up systems
D. Reducing data

Who is responsible for AI decisions?
A. Machines
B. Humans

C. Robots
D. No one

Why is trust important in AI?
A. It is not important
B. It makes AI faster
C. It ensures people accept and use AI
D. It removes data

What is accountability?
A. Ignoring results
B. Taking responsibility for outcomes
C. Avoiding decisions
D. Speeding up AI

Why can AI not make ethical decisions alone?
A. It is too slow
B. It lacks human values and judgment
C. It has emotions
D. It stops working

What is one risk of unethical AI?
A. Better performance
B. Fair decisions
C. Harmful or unfair outcomes
D. Faster results

What is the main idea of this chapter?
A. AI does not need ethics
B. AI should replace humans
C. Ethics and responsibility guide AI use
D. AI is always correct

Answer Key

Worksheet Part A:

D

C

E

B

A

Quiz Answers:

C

B

C

B

B

C

B

B

C

C

CHAPTER 20 The Legacy of ANI — Humanity's First Step Toward Conscious Technology

Introduction

Every great journey begins with a single step.
For humanity's journey into artificial intelligence, that step was **Artificial Narrow Intelligence (ANI)** — the first form of machine learning capable of performing tasks once thought to require the human mind.

From digital assistants to medical algorithms, ANI has become a silent companion in nearly every aspect of modern life.
It reads, listens, drives, translates, and predicts.
But its true legacy lies not in what it can do — it lies in what it has *taught humanity about itself.*

This chapter looks back at the impact of ANI, the lessons it leaves behind, and the foundation it builds for the age of **Artificial General Intelligence (AGI)** and beyond.

The First Generation of Machine Intelligence

Artificial Narrow Intelligence marked the beginning of conscious technology — not conscious in the human sense, but advanced enough to perceive, learn, and respond.
It represented the birth of systems that could analyze information faster and more accurately than the human brain in specific fields.

For example, AI is used in schools to help students learn, in hospitals to assist doctors in diagnosing illnesses, and in businesses to improve customer service. These tools show how AI can support human work—but they still require human oversight." This first generation of intelligent machines introduced three revolutions:

1. **Automation of Knowledge Work:** Tasks once requiring mental effort — calculations, sorting, analysis — became automated.
2. **Integration into Daily Life:** From smartphones to cars, ANI entered every home, classroom, and workplace.
3. **Reflection of Humanity:** Through its limitations, ANI revealed the depth and complexity of human emotion, creativity, and morality.

In these ways, ANI became more than a tool; it became humanity's mirror — showing both the brilliance and responsibility of intelligence.

A Mirror of Human Intellect

When machines learned to imitate aspects of human thought, humanity began to understand its own intelligence more deeply.
We learned that intelligence is not only logic, but emotion.

Not only speed, but empathy.
Not only memory, but imagination.

Every algorithm that mimics perception or language has taught scientists how humans think, remember, and decide.
Through ANI, neuroscience, psychology, and education have advanced together — revealing that learning, whether biological or artificial, follows the same universal principle: feedback, reflection, and growth.

This realization reshaped the meaning of intelligence — transforming it from a competition into a collaboration.

Teaching Machines, Teaching Ourselves

When people teach machines to learn, they also learn about themselves.
By training ANI, we discover our patterns, our values, and our blind spots.
If a system reproduces bias, it reflects our own.
If it amplifies creativity, it reflects our potential.

In this sense, ANI is both a student and a teacher — learning from humanity and teaching humanity in return.
It shows us that the development of technology is also the development of character.
Each dataset becomes a moral decision, and every algorithm becomes a statement of who we are as a civilization.

Ethics as the Core of Legacy

The legacy of ANI is not measured in speed or efficiency, but in *ethics*.
It has forced humanity to ask timeless questions in new forms:

- What is fairness in a world ruled by data?
- How do we protect privacy when knowledge becomes infinite?
- Can machines make moral decisions, or do they only reflect ours?

Through these questions, society has begun to shape a new ethical compass for the digital age — one that values transparency, accountability, and compassion.
The real inheritance of ANI is not technology; it is *wisdom*.

Bridging Generations of Intelligence

ANI stands as the bridge between mechanical computation and cognitive understanding.
It is the foundation upon which **AGI** — Artificial General Intelligence — will rise.
Without ANI's narrow focus, there could be no broad intelligence to come.

Just as early machines taught humanity how to measure and compute, ANI has taught us how to teach and reflect.
Its systems have become laboratories of thought, preparing both humans and machines for a more unified future.

Teachers can use this chapter to remind students that progress is built step by step — one invention leading to another, one discovery preparing the next.
In the history of AI, ANI is not a chapter to be closed, but one to be remembered as the beginning of the great unfolding story of consciousness.

The Human Element That Endures

No matter how advanced technology becomes, one truth remains: machines may simulate thought, but they cannot feel purpose.
Humanity's role is to give direction to intelligence — to ensure it serves life, not replaces it.

The endurance of compassion, creativity, and moral courage defines the soul of progress.
As ANI continues to evolve, these values must remain the compass guiding every algorithm and every innovation.
Only when guided by heart and wisdom can intelligence — artificial or otherwise — uplift the world rather than divide it.

Preparing for Conscious Technology

As we move toward AGI and eventually **Artificial Superintelligence (ASI)**, society must remember what ANI has taught: that intelligence without ethics is power without peace.
The next stage of evolution will not depend on faster computers, but on wiser creators.

Conscious technology begins not when machines awaken — but when humanity does.
It begins when people understand that intelligence is not just about solving problems, but about serving a greater purpose.

ANI has given us the tools to reach that horizon; what we build there will define the legacy of the human race.

The Legacy of Learning

For teachers, this chapter closes the first level of understanding.
For students, it opens the next.
Artificial Narrow Intelligence is no longer just a subject — it is a part of daily life and global identity.

Its legacy can be summarized in three lessons:

1. **Intelligence is shared.**
   No system learns alone — humans and machines grow together.
2. **Ethics is essential.**
   Without moral guidance, intelligence loses its meaning.
3. **Humanity is irreplaceable.**
   Technology extends ability, but only humanity gives it soul.

If these lessons are remembered, ANI will be known not just as the birth of artificial thought, but as the *awakening of human responsibility.*

Conclusion

The story of Artificial Narrow Intelligence is a story of beginnings — the dawn of a new era where machines learn, humans reflect, and intelligence itself evolves.
It is the first light of a future filled with possibility, challenge, and hope.

Its true legacy will not be measured in devices or data, but in the wisdom humanity gains through its creation.
ANI has shown that intelligence is not about competition between human and machine — it is about cooperation toward understanding.

For teachers, this final chapter is a reminder that education must always lead technology.
For students, it is a call to build the future not with fear, but with faith — faith in learning, in compassion, and in the enduring brilliance of the human mind.

Artificial Narrow Intelligence was humanity's first conversation with itself through technology
—
and it is a conversation that will echo through every generation to come.

Imagine a future where students work alongside AI to solve global challenges such as climate change, disease, and education inequality.

CHAPTER 20 – TEACHER & STUDENT MATERIALS

The Future of AI — Leadership, Responsibility, and Human Potential

Extended Summary

This chapter serves as a powerful conclusion to the study of Artificial Intelligence by focusing on the future and the role that students will play in shaping it. As AI continues to evolve, it is becoming deeply integrated into everyday life—impacting education, healthcare, business, communication, and decision-making.

Students learn that AI is not just a technological advancement but a human responsibility. While machines can process data, recognize patterns, and automate tasks, they cannot replace human values such as empathy, ethics, creativity, and moral judgment. The future of AI will depend not on how advanced machines become, but on how wisely humans guide their development.

The chapter emphasizes that the next generation must be prepared not only with technical knowledge but also with strong character and critical thinking skills. Students are encouraged to become leaders who understand both the power and limitations of AI. They must learn to ask important questions: Is this technology fair? Is it safe? Does it benefit society?

Leadership in the age of AI means taking responsibility for how technology is used. This includes designing systems that are inclusive, ethical, and beneficial for all people. It also means recognizing that mistakes can happen and being willing to improve systems over time.

The chapter highlights that education is the foundation for this future. Schools must prepare students to think independently, solve complex problems, and collaborate with intelligent systems. Students should not fear AI, but instead understand it and use it as a tool to improve the world.

In conclusion, the future of AI is not determined by machines—it is shaped by people. Students are not just observers of this transformation; they are active participants. By developing knowledge, responsibility, and leadership, they can ensure that AI becomes a force for good in society.

Reflection

What does it mean to be a leader in an AI-driven world?

Why can AI not replace human values such as empathy and ethics?

How can students use AI responsibly in their daily lives?

What skills are most important for the future of AI?

Why is education important in preparing students for AI?

How can AI benefit society when used correctly?

What risks exist if AI is not guided properly?

How can students become responsible users of technology?

What role do humans play in shaping the future of AI?

What kind of future do you want AI to help create?

Worksheet

Part A: Vocabulary Matching

A. Leadership
B. Ethics
C. Artificial Intelligence
D. Responsibility
E. Critical Thinking

___ Making decisions based on moral values

___ Technology that simulates human intelligence

___ Taking ownership of actions and outcomes

___ Guiding others toward a goal

___ Analyzing and evaluating information carefully

Part B: Short Answer

What is one way AI is used in everyday life?

Why is human responsibility important in AI development?

Name one skill students need for the future.

What does ethical AI mean?

Why is critical thinking important when using AI?

Part C: Critical Thinking

Write a paragraph (5–7 sentences):

Explain how students can become leaders in an AI-driven future. Include both skills and responsibilities.

Quiz (10 Questions)

What is the main idea of Chapter 20?
A. AI will replace all humans
B. Students must lead and guide the future of AI
C. AI is not important
D. Technology should be avoided

Why are human values important in AI?
A. Machines have values
B. AI can think emotionally
C. Humans provide ethics and judgment
D. AI replaces humans

What is one role of students in the future of AI?
A. Ignore technology
B. Become responsible leaders
C. Avoid learning
D. Replace machines

What does ethical AI mean?
A. Fast AI
B. Expensive AI
C. Fair and responsible use of AI
D. Automatic AI

Why is critical thinking important?
A. To avoid learning
B. To question and evaluate AI outputs

C. To replace AI
D. To stop technology

What is one benefit of AI?
A. It removes all jobs
B. It helps solve problems efficiently
C. It replaces education
D. It stops thinking

What is one risk of AI?
A. It never works
B. It can be misused without guidance
C. It cannot learn
D. It has no impact

What skill is important for the future?
A. Ignoring AI
B. Creativity and problem-solving
C. Avoiding technology
D. Memorization only

Who is responsible for how AI is used?
A. Only machines
B. Only companies
C. Humans
D. No one

What is the key message of the chapter?
A. AI controls the future
B. Humans shape the future of AI
C. AI replaces leadership
D. AI stops learning

Answer Key

Worksheet Part A:

B

C

D

A

E

Quiz Answers:

B

C

B

C

B

B

B

B

C

B

GLOSSARY

Letter A

1. Access Time

The amount of time it takes for an AI system or computer to locate and retrieve data from memory or storage. Access time affects how quickly megabytes of data can be used during AI processing.

2. Activation Data

Intermediate data generated inside an AI model while it is running. Activation data is stored temporarily in memory and often measured in megabytes during model execution.

3. Adaptive Storage

A storage approach that automatically adjusts how data is stored or moved based on usage patterns. In AI systems, adaptive storage helps manage large volumes of megabytes efficiently.

4. Algorithmic Data Size

The total amount of data an algorithm needs to operate effectively. In AI, this size is often measured in megabytes or larger units, depending on model complexity.

5. Allocation (Memory Allocation)

The process of assigning a specific number of megabytes in memory or storage for an AI task, model, or dataset.

6. Analytics Dataset

A structured collection of data used for analysis or AI training. The size of an analytics dataset is commonly measured in megabytes, gigabytes, or more.

7. Annotation Storage

The space required to store labels, tags, or explanations added to AI training data. These annotations contribute additional megabytes to total dataset size.

8. Artificial Neural Network (ANN) Size

The total memory footprint of a neural network, including weights, biases, and parameters. ANN size is often described in megabytes when discussing model efficiency.

9. Asset Compression

The process of reducing the number of megabytes required to store AI-related files such as models, images, or datasets without losing essential information.

10. Available Memory

The amount of free memory, measured in megabytes, that an AI system can still use to load data, run models, or perform computations.

ANI (Artificial Narrow Intelligence)

Artificial Narrow Intelligence refers to AI systems designed to perform **one specific task or a narrow set of tasks** rather than general intelligence. ANI systems rely on data stored and processed in memory and storage measured in **megabytes, gigabytes, or more**. Examples include image recognition, speech-to-text, recommendation systems, and chatbots. ANI does not understand beyond its training scope, but it can process large amounts of data efficiently within its defined function.

Letter B

1. Bandwidth

The amount of data that can be transferred between systems in a given time. In AI systems, bandwidth determines how quickly megabytes of data can move between storage, memory, and processors.

2. Batch Processing

A method where AI systems process large groups of data all at once instead of one item at a time. Batch processing often involves handling many megabytes of data in a single operation.

3. Binary Encoding

The process of representing information using binary values (0s and 1s). All megabytes of AI data are ultimately stored and transmitted using binary encoding.

4. Bit Depth

The number of bits used to represent a single piece of data, such as a pixel or audio sample. Higher bit depth increases data quality but also increases the number of megabytes required.

5. Bitmap Data

A type of image data where each pixel is stored as a set of bits. Bitmap images can quickly grow in size, consuming large numbers of megabytes in AI vision systems.

6. Buffer Memory

Temporary memory used to hold data while it is being transferred or processed. Buffers store data in chunks measured in megabytes to keep AI systems running smoothly.

7. Bulk Data Storage

Large-scale storage designed to hold massive datasets used for AI training or analysis. Bulk storage capacity is measured in megabytes, gigabytes, or larger units.

8. Byte Stream

A continuous flow of bytes transmitted or processed by a system. AI applications often analyze byte streams that accumulate into megabytes of data.

9. Bytecode

An intermediate form of program code that is easier for machines to execute than human-written code. Bytecode files occupy storage space measured in megabytes.

10. Byzantine Fault Tolerance (BFT)

A system property that allows AI or distributed systems to continue functioning even when some components fail or act unpredictably. Implementing BFT requires additional data handling and storage overhead measured in megabytes.

Letter C

1. Cache Memory

A small, high-speed memory area that stores frequently used data so the processor can access it faster. Cache helps reduce the time needed to move megabytes of data from main memory or storage.

2. Capacity Planning

The process of estimating how much memory and storage an AI system will need. Capacity planning ensures there are enough megabytes available to handle data, models, and future growth.

3. Checkpoint File

A saved snapshot of an AI model during training. Checkpoint files are stored in memory or storage and often consume many megabytes so training can resume without starting over.

4. Chunking

The practice of breaking large datasets into smaller pieces. Chunking helps AI systems process megabytes of data more efficiently by handling them in manageable parts.

5. Cloud Storage

A method of storing data on remote servers accessed through the internet. Cloud storage manages files measured in megabytes and allows AI systems to scale beyond local hardware limits.

6. Compression

The process of reducing the size of data so it uses fewer megabytes. Compression helps AI systems store, transfer, and process data more efficiently.

7. Compute Load

The amount of processing work required to run an AI task. Compute load often increases as the number of megabytes being processed grows.

8. Context Window

The amount of data an AI model can consider at one time. Context windows consume memory measured in megabytes, especially in language and vision models.

9. Corpus

A large collection of text or data used to train AI models. A corpus is usually measured in megabytes or larger units depending on its size.

10. CUDA Memory

Specialized memory used by GPUs to accelerate AI computations. CUDA memory holds model data and intermediate results measured in megabytes during processing.

Letter D

1. Data Allocation

The process of assigning a specific amount of memory or storage for data use. In AI systems, data allocation determines how many megabytes are reserved for datasets, models, or tasks.

2. Data Buffer

A temporary storage area that holds data while it is being transferred or processed. Data buffers manage megabytes of information to keep AI systems running smoothly.

3. Data Compression

A technique used to reduce the size of data so it consumes fewer megabytes. AI systems use data compression to save storage space and speed up data transfer.

4. Data Footprint

The total amount of data an AI system uses, including datasets, models, and temporary files. A data footprint is measured in megabytes, gigabytes, or more.

5. Data Loader

A software component that loads data into memory for AI training or inference. Data loaders handle batches of data measured in megabytes.

6. Data Migration

The process of moving data from one storage system to another. During AI system upgrades, data migration may involve transferring large numbers of megabytes.

7. Data Throughput

The rate at which data is processed or transferred by a system. Higher throughput allows AI systems to move more megabytes efficiently.

8. Dataset Size

The total amount of data in a dataset used for AI training or testing. Dataset size is commonly measured in megabytes or larger units.

9. Deep Learning Model Size

The amount of memory required to store a deep learning model, including its parameters and weights. Model size is often described in megabytes to assess efficiency.

10. Disk Storage

Long-term storage used to save files, datasets, and AI models. Disk storage capacity and usage are measured in megabytes, gigabytes, or terabytes.

Letter E

1. Edge Computing

A computing approach where data is processed closer to where it is generated rather than sent to a central server. Edge computing reduces how many megabytes must be transferred over networks.

2. Embedding Size

The amount of memory required to store vector representations used by AI models. Embedding size is often measured in megabytes and affects model performance and storage needs.

3. Encoded Data

Data that has been converted into a specific format for storage or transmission. Encoded data occupies megabytes depending on the encoding method used.

4. Encoding Scheme

A rule set that defines how data is represented digitally, such as text or images. Different encoding schemes can increase or reduce the number of megabytes required.

5. Encrypted Storage

Storage that protects data by converting it into a secure format. Encryption may slightly increase the number of megabytes used due to added security information.

6. End-to-End Data Pipeline

The full path data takes from collection to processing and storage. Each stage of the pipeline manages data volumes measured in megabytes.

7. Energy Efficiency (AI Systems)

A measure of how much energy an AI system uses to process data. Systems that move and store fewer megabytes are often more energy efficient.

8. Execution Memory

The memory required while a program or AI model is running. Execution memory usage is tracked in megabytes during runtime.

9. External Storage

Storage devices located outside a computer, such as USB drives or external hard drives. External storage capacity is measured in megabytes and larger units.

10. Extracted Features

Important data patterns identified by AI models during processing. Extracted features are stored temporarily or permanently in memory measured in megabytes.

Letter F

1. Feature Map

A structured output produced by AI models, especially in image and signal processing. Feature maps are stored in memory and can consume significant megabytes during computation.

2. Feature Scaling

The process of adjusting data values to a consistent range before training an AI model. Feature scaling affects how efficiently megabytes of data are processed and stored.

3. File Allocation Table (FAT)

A file system structure that tracks where files are stored on a disk. FAT helps manage how megabytes are organized and retrieved from storage.

4. File Compression Format

A standardized way to reduce file size so it uses fewer megabytes. Compression formats help AI systems store and transfer data efficiently.

5. File System Cache

A temporary memory area that stores frequently accessed files. File system caches reduce repeated access to storage and manage megabytes more efficiently.

6. Floating-Point Data

Numerical data that includes decimal values and is commonly used in AI calculations. Floating-point data requires more bits per value, increasing memory usage measured in megabytes.

7. Frame Buffer

A region of memory that stores image or video frames before they are displayed or processed. Frame buffers often consume large numbers of megabytes in AI vision systems.

8. Fragmentation

A condition where data is stored in scattered locations instead of one continuous block. Fragmentation can reduce storage efficiency even when megabytes appear available.

9. Free Memory

The amount of unused memory available for programs or AI tasks. Free memory is measured in megabytes and determines how much additional data can be loaded.

10. Full Dataset Load

The act of loading an entire dataset into memory at once. This approach can require large amounts of megabytes and is common in AI training scenarios.

Letter G

1. Garbage Collection

An automatic memory-management process that frees memory no longer in use. Garbage collection helps reclaim megabytes so AI programs can continue running efficiently.

2. Generalization Data

Data used to test how well an AI model performs on new, unseen inputs. Storing and evaluating generalization data requires additional megabytes beyond training data.

3. Gigabyte (GB)

A larger unit of data measurement equal to 1,024 megabytes (or commonly approximated as 1,000 MB). Gigabytes are used when datasets or models grow beyond megabyte scale.

4. Graph Data Structure

A way of organizing data using nodes and connections. Graph-based AI systems store graph data in memory and storage measured in megabytes.

5. GPU Memory

Specialized memory used by graphics processing units to accelerate AI workloads. GPU memory holds model parameters and data batches measured in megabytes.

6. Gradient Data

Numerical values calculated during AI training to update model parameters. Gradient data is stored temporarily in memory and contributes to overall megabyte usage.

7. Granularity

The level of detail at which data is stored or processed. Finer granularity often increases the number of megabytes required.

8. Greedy Algorithm

An algorithm that makes the best immediate choice at each step. Greedy algorithms may reduce memory usage by limiting how many megabytes of data must be stored at once.

9. Ground Truth Data

Correct, labeled data used to train or evaluate AI systems. Ground truth datasets are stored in files measured in megabytes or larger units.

10. Growth Rate (Data)

The speed at which data size increases over time. In AI systems, a high data growth rate means storage needs measured in megabytes can expand quickly.

Letter H

1. Hard Disk Capacity

The total amount of data a hard disk can store. Capacity is measured in megabytes and larger units.

2. Hardware Acceleration

The use of specialized hardware to speed up AI processing. Acceleration often reduces how long megabytes of data stay in memory.

3. Hash Table

A data structure that stores information for fast lookup. Hash tables occupy memory measured in megabytes in large AI systems.

4. Hierarchical Storage

A storage design that uses multiple layers such as RAM, disk, and cloud. Each layer manages data measured in megabytes.

5. High-Dimensional Data

Data with many features or variables. High-dimensional datasets often require large numbers of megabytes.

6. Host Memory

Main system memory used by the CPU. Host memory stores AI data and models measured in megabytes.

7. Hybrid Storage

A combination of different storage types working together. Hybrid storage systems manage megabytes across multiple devices.

8. Hyperparameter Storage

Memory used to store configuration values for AI models. These settings are saved in files measured in megabytes.

9. Hyperscale Data

Extremely large datasets used by major AI systems. Hyperscale data is tracked from megabytes up to much larger units.

10. Heuristic Data

Information used by AI systems to guide decision-making. Heuristic data contributes to the overall data size in megabytes.

Letter I

1. Image Dataset Size

The total amount of storage required for image data. Size is measured in megabytes or more.

2. Inference Memory

The memory used when an AI model is making predictions. Inference memory usage is tracked in megabytes.

3. Input Buffer

A temporary area where incoming data is stored. Input buffers hold megabytes before processing begins.

4. Intermediate Data

Data produced during processing steps. Intermediate data can significantly increase memory usage in megabytes.

5. Index File

A file that helps locate data quickly. Index files use additional megabytes to improve performance.

6. Information Density

The amount of useful data stored within a given size. Higher density means more information per megabyte.

7. Initialization Data

Data loaded when an AI system starts. Initialization data occupies memory measured in megabytes.

8. In-Memory Processing

Processing data directly in RAM instead of storage. This approach uses large amounts of memory measured in megabytes.

9. Input Feature Size

The amount of data required to represent input features. Feature size affects how many megabytes are needed.

10. Instruction Cache

A small memory area that stores frequently used instructions. Instruction caches manage small but critical megabytes.

Letter J

1. Job Queue

A list of tasks waiting to be processed. Job queues may store task data measured in megabytes.

2. Joint Dataset

A dataset created by combining multiple sources. Joint datasets often increase total size in megabytes.

3. JSON Data Size

The amount of storage required for data stored in JSON format. JSON files can grow quickly in megabytes.

4. Jitter Buffer

A temporary storage area that smooths data flow. Jitter buffers store megabytes during real-time processing.

5. Job Scheduler

A system that decides when tasks run. Schedulers manage memory and data measured in megabytes.

6. Just-in-Time Processing

Processing data only when needed. This approach can reduce how many megabytes are stored at once.

7. Joint Memory Allocation

Memory shared across multiple AI tasks. Joint allocation must carefully manage available megabytes.

8. Java Bytecode Size

The storage size of compiled Java programs. Bytecode files occupy megabytes on disk.

9. Job Metadata

Information describing AI tasks. Metadata adds additional megabytes to total system storage.

10. Junction Storage Point

A logical link between storage locations. Junctions help organize data measured in megabytes.

Letter K

1. Kernel Memory

Memory reserved for core system operations. Kernel memory usage is tracked in megabytes.

2. Key-Value Store

A data storage method that pairs keys with values. Large key-value stores consume many megabytes.

3. Knowledge Base Size

The total amount of stored knowledge in an AI system. Size is measured in megabytes or larger units.

4. K-Means Dataset Size

The amount of data used in clustering algorithms. Dataset size affects memory usage in megabytes.

5. Keras Model Size

The storage required for AI models built with Keras. Model size is measured in megabytes.

6. Keyframe Data

Important frames selected from video data. Keyframe storage contributes to total megabyte usage.

7. Kernel Cache

A cache used by the operating system kernel. Kernel caches store frequently used data in megabytes.

8. Knowledge Graph Storage

Memory used to store relationships between data points. Knowledge graphs require significant megabytes.

9. Kinetic Data Stream

Continuously changing data from sensors or systems. These streams generate growing megabytes over time.

10. K-Nearest Neighbor Memory Usage

The memory required by nearest-neighbor algorithms. Memory use increases as datasets grow in megabytes.

Letter L

1. **Latency**
   The delay between requesting data and receiving it. Latency affects how quickly megabytes move through AI systems.
2. **Layer Output Size**
   The amount of data produced by a neural network layer. Output size is measured in megabytes during processing.
3. **Load Balancing**
   Distributing work across systems so no single device is overloaded. Balancing helps manage megabytes efficiently.
4. **Local Storage**
   Data stored on a device rather than the cloud. Local storage capacity is measured in megabytes.
5. **Log File Size**
   The amount of storage used by system logs. Logs can accumulate many megabytes over time.
6. **Loss History Data**
   Stored values showing how model error changes during training. Loss history consumes megabytes.
7. **Low-Precision Data**
   Data stored using fewer bits per value. Low-precision formats reduce megabyte usage.
8. **Labeled Dataset**
   Data that includes tags or labels for AI training. Labels increase total dataset size in megabytes.
9. **Linear Model Size**
   The storage required for a linear AI model. Size is measured in megabytes.
10. **Load Time**
    The time required to bring data or models into memory. Load time depends on megabytes involved.

Letter M

1. **Memory Allocation**
   Assigning a specific amount of memory for tasks. Allocation is tracked in megabytes.
2. **Memory Footprint**
   The total memory an AI program uses. Footprint is measured in megabytes.
3. **Metadata Size**
   The storage used by descriptive information about data. Metadata adds extra megabytes.
4. **Mini-Batch Size**
   The amount of data processed at once during training. Batch size affects megabyte usage.

5. **Model Checkpoint Size**
   The storage required for saved training states. Checkpoints often consume many megabytes.
6. **Model Compression**
   Reducing model size while preserving performance. Compression lowers megabytes required.
7. **Model Parameters**
   Values learned by an AI model. Parameter storage contributes to total megabytes.
8. **Memory Bandwidth**
   The rate at which memory transfers data. Bandwidth affects how fast megabytes move.
9. **Multimodal Dataset**
   Data combining text, images, audio, or video. Multimodal data uses large megabytes.
10. **Mutable Data**
    Data that changes during processing. Mutable data can increase temporary megabyte usage.

Letter N

1. **Network Bandwidth**
   The capacity of a network connection. Bandwidth controls how many megabytes can be transferred.
2. **Neural Network Size**
   The total storage required for a neural network. Size is measured in megabytes.
3. **Node Memory**
   Memory available on a computing node. Node memory limits megabytes per task.
4. **Normalization Data**
   Values used to scale data consistently. Normalization adds to dataset megabytes.
5. **Non-Volatile Memory**
   Memory that retains data without power. Capacity is measured in megabytes.
6. **Numerical Precision**
   The detail level of stored numbers. Higher precision increases megabytes.
7. **Noise Data**
   Unwanted or random information in datasets. Noise increases data size in megabytes.
8. **Neural Activation Size**
   Memory used to store neuron outputs. Activation size is measured in megabytes.
9. **Network Transfer Size**
   The amount of data sent across a network. Transfer size is tracked in megabytes.
10. **Node Cache**
    Temporary storage on a node for faster access. Cache size uses megabytes.

Letter O

1. **Object Storage**
   A storage method that manages data as objects. Capacity is measured in megabytes.
2. **Offline Dataset**
   Data stored locally rather than streamed. Offline datasets occupy megabytes.
3. **On-Device Storage**
   Storage located on the AI device itself. On-device capacity is measured in megabytes.
4. **Operational Memory**
   Memory used during active AI operations. Usage is tracked in megabytes.
5. **Optimization Data**
   Information used to improve model performance. Optimization data uses megabytes.
6. **Output Buffer**
   Temporary storage for results before delivery. Buffers hold megabytes.
7. **Overhead Data**
   Extra data required for system operation. Overhead increases total megabytes.
8. **Object Detection Output Size**
   The amount of data produced by detection models. Output size is measured in megabytes.
9. **Online Storage**
   Storage accessible via the internet. Online storage limits are measured in megabytes.
10. **Open Dataset Size**
    The storage footprint of publicly available datasets. Size is measured in megabytes.

Letter P

1. **Parameter Count**
   The total number of model values. Count correlates with megabytes required.
2. **Persistent Storage**
   Long-term storage that retains data. Capacity is measured in megabytes.
3. **Pipeline Buffer**
   Temporary storage between processing stages. Buffers manage megabytes in motion.
4. **Preprocessing Data**
   Data created while preparing datasets. Preprocessing adds megabytes.
5. **Precision Reduction**
   Lowering numeric detail to save space. Reduction decreases megabyte usage.
6. **Prediction Output Size**
   The amount of data produced by model predictions. Size is measured in megabytes.
7. **Primary Memory**
   Main system memory used for processing. Capacity is measured in megabytes.
8. **Processing Overhead**
   Extra resources needed during computation. Overhead increases megabyte usage.
9. **Profiling Data**
   Information collected to analyze performance. Profiling data uses megabytes.
10. **Paged Memory**
    Memory divided into fixed-size blocks. Paging manages megabytes efficiently.

Letter Q

1. **Quantization**
   A technique that reduces numerical precision to lower memory usage. Quantization helps AI models use fewer megabytes.
2. **Query Cache**
   Stored results from previous searches or requests. Query caches save megabytes by avoiding repeated computation.
3. **Query Latency**
   The time it takes to retrieve data after a request. Latency depends on how many megabytes must be accessed.
4. **Queue Buffer**
   A temporary holding area for data waiting to be processed. Buffers store megabytes in order.
5. **Quick Access Memory**
   Memory designed for fast retrieval. It handles megabytes needed immediately by AI tasks.
6. **Quantitative Dataset**
   Data made up of numerical values. These datasets are stored and measured in megabytes.
7. **Query Result Size**
   The amount of data returned from a query. Result size is measured in megabytes.
8. **Quorum Storage**
   A distributed storage method requiring agreement across systems. Data is replicated in megabytes.
9. **Quality Metrics Data**
   Information used to measure model performance. Metrics consume storage in megabytes.
10. **Quantized Model Size**
    The reduced size of an AI model after quantization. Size is typically measured in megabytes.

Letter R

1. **RAM Usage**
   The amount of active memory in use. RAM usage is tracked in megabytes.
2. **Read Throughput**
   The speed at which data is read from storage. Throughput affects how fast megabytes are accessed.
3. **Real-Time Processing**
   Processing data immediately as it arrives. Real-time systems manage megabytes continuously.
4. **Recursive Memory Use**
   Memory consumption during repeated function calls. Usage accumulates in megabytes.

5. **Redundant Storage**
   Extra copies of data kept for reliability. Redundancy increases total megabytes stored.
6. **Resource Allocation**
   Assigning system resources like memory and storage. Allocation is measured in megabytes.
7. **Runtime Memory**
   Memory required while a program is running. Runtime memory usage is tracked in megabytes.
8. **Raw Dataset Size**
   The size of unprocessed data. Raw datasets often require many megabytes.
9. **Read-Only Memory Footprint**
   The storage space used by non-modifiable data. Footprint is measured in megabytes.
10. **Retrieval Speed**
    How quickly stored data can be accessed. Speed depends on the number of megabytes involved.

Letter S

1. **Sample Size**
   The number of data examples used in AI training. Larger samples increase megabytes.
2. **Scalable Storage**
   Storage that grows with demand. Scalability supports increasing megabytes.
3. **Serialized Data Size**
   The storage size of data converted into a transferable format. Size is measured in megabytes.
4. **Shared Memory**
   Memory accessible by multiple processes. Shared memory usage is tracked in megabytes.
5. **Snapshot Size**
   The storage required for saved system states. Snapshots consume megabytes.
6. **Sparse Data Representation**
   A storage method that saves space when data contains many empty values. Sparsity reduces megabytes.
7. **Storage Capacity**
   The total amount of data a system can store. Capacity is measured in megabytes or more.
8. **Streaming Data Buffer**
   Temporary storage for incoming data streams. Buffers handle megabytes in motion.
9. **System Cache**
   Memory that stores frequently used data. Caches manage megabytes for faster access.
10. **Synchronization Data**
    Information used to keep systems aligned. Sync data adds to total megabytes.

Letter T

1. **Temporary Storage**
   Short-term storage used during processing. Temporary storage holds megabytes briefly.
2. **Tensor Size**
   The memory required to store multidimensional data structures. Tensor size is measured in megabytes.
3. **Throughput Rate**
   The amount of data processed per unit time. Rate is often described in megabytes per second.
4. **Training Dataset Size**
   The total amount of data used to train AI models. Size is measured in megabytes.
5. **Transfer Buffer**
   Temporary memory used during data movement. Buffers hold megabytes during transfer.
6. **Transactional Storage**
   Storage that ensures data consistency. Transactions add overhead measured in megabytes.
7. **Thread Memory Usage**
   Memory consumed by execution threads. Usage is tracked in megabytes.
8. **Token Storage Size**
   The memory required to store processed tokens. Token data uses megabytes.
9. **Time-Series Data Size**
   The storage footprint of data collected over time. Size increases in megabytes.
10. **Training Checkpoint Size**
    The storage required for saved training states. Checkpoints are measured in megabytes.

Letter U

1. **Unified Memory**
   A memory system shared between CPU and GPU. Unified memory manages data in megabytes efficiently across processors.
2. **Upload Size**
   The amount of data sent to storage or the cloud. Upload size is measured in megabytes.
3. **User Data Storage**
   Storage allocated for user-generated files. Capacity is tracked in megabytes.
4. **Utilization Rate**
   The percentage of memory or storage currently in use. Utilization reflects how many megabytes are occupied.
5. **Uncompressed Data Size**
   The size of data before compression. Uncompressed data often uses more megabytes.
6. **Update Payload**
   Data sent during software or model updates. Payload size is measured in megabytes.
7. **Uptime Storage Logs**
   Logs recorded while systems run continuously. Logs accumulate megabytes over time.
8. **Unified Dataset**
   A dataset combined from multiple sources. Size is measured in megabytes.

9. **User Session Memory**
   Memory allocated for active users. Session memory uses megabytes dynamically.
10. **Usage Quota**
   A storage limit set for users or systems. Quotas are defined in megabytes or larger units.

Letter V

1. **Validation Dataset Size**
   The amount of data used to evaluate AI models. Size is measured in megabytes.
2. **Vector Embedding Size**
   The memory required to store numerical representations of data. Size is measured in megabytes.
3. **Virtual Memory**
   A system that extends RAM using disk storage. Virtual memory is managed in megabytes.
4. **Volatile Memory**
   Memory that loses data when power is off. Capacity is measured in megabytes.
5. **Video Dataset Size**
   The storage required for video data. Video datasets consume many megabytes.
6. **Versioned Storage**
   Storage that keeps multiple file versions. Versioning increases megabyte usage.
7. **Vision Model Size**
   The memory footprint of computer vision models. Size is measured in megabytes.
8. **Vector Database Storage**
   Storage used for similarity search data. Vector databases consume large megabytes.
9. **Virtualized Storage**
   Storage abstracted from physical hardware. Capacity is tracked in megabytes.
10. **Volume Capacity**
   The total size of a storage volume. Capacity is measured in megabytes or more.

Letter W

1. **Weight Parameters**
   Learned values in AI models. Weight storage contributes to megabytes used.
2. **Working Memory**
   Memory actively used during processing. Working memory usage is measured in megabytes.
3. **Write Throughput**
   The speed at which data is written to storage. Throughput affects megabytes per second.
4. **Warm Cache**
   Cached data that is already loaded. Warm caches reduce repeated megabyte transfers.

5. **Workflow Data Size**
   The total data used across an AI workflow. Size is measured in megabytes.
6. **Web Dataset Size**
   The storage required for web-based data. Size is tracked in megabytes.
7. **Weight Compression**
   Reducing model weight size to save memory. Compression lowers megabytes used.
8. **Window Size (AI Context)**
   The amount of data processed at once. Window size affects memory megabytes.
9. **Writable Storage**
   Storage that allows data modification. Capacity is measured in megabytes.
10. **Workload Memory Demand**
   The memory required for tasks. Demand is expressed in megabytes.

Letter X

1. **X-Axis Data Size**
   Data stored along one dimension of a dataset. Size contributes to megabytes used.
2. **XML Data Size**
   The storage footprint of XML-formatted data. XML files often use many megabytes.
3. **XOR Encoding**
   A binary operation used in data processing. Encoded data occupies megabytes.
4. **Execution Context Size**
   Memory required during task execution. Size is measured in megabytes.
5. **External Dataset Size**
   The size of data sourced externally. External datasets add megabytes.
6. **Expanded Memory Use**
   Memory growth during processing. Expansion increases megabytes consumed.
7. **Experimental Dataset**
   Data used for testing AI models. Size is measured in megabytes.
8. **Extraction Buffer**
   Temporary storage during data extraction. Buffers store megabytes briefly.
9. **Extended Storage Capacity**
   Additional storage added to a system. Capacity is measured in megabytes.
10. **Explainability Data Size**
   Data used to explain AI decisions. Explainability outputs consume megabytes.

Letter Y

1. **Yield Data Size**
   The amount of useful output data produced. Yield is measured in megabytes.
2. **Yearly Data Growth**
   Annual increase in stored data. Growth is tracked in megabytes.

3. **YAML File Size**
   The storage footprint of YAML configuration files. Size is measured in megabytes.
4. **Y-Axis Feature Size**
   Feature data along a dataset dimension. Size contributes to megabytes.
5. **Young Generation Memory**
   Memory area for newly created data. Usage is measured in megabytes.
6. **Yield Optimization Data**
   Data used to improve output efficiency. Stored in megabytes.
7. **YourAIStudyBuddy Dataset Size**
   The total data used by AI study tools. Size is measured in megabytes.
8. **Yottabyte Reference Scale**
   A conceptual upper scale of data measurement. Used for comparison beyond megabytes.
9. **Yield Metrics Storage**
   Storage used for performance metrics. Metrics consume megabytes.
10. **Yoked Memory Allocation**
    Linked memory regions used together. Allocation is measured in megabytes.

Letter Z

1. **Zero-Copy Memory**
   A method that avoids duplicating data. Zero-copy reduces megabytes in motion.
2. **Zipped Dataset Size**
   The storage size after compression. Zipped files use fewer megabytes.
3. **Zettabyte Scale (Reference)**
   A large-scale data concept. Used to compare growth beyond megabytes.
4. **Zone-Based Storage**
   Storage divided into regions. Zones manage megabytes efficiently.
5. **Z-Score Normalization Data**
   Statistical values used in preprocessing. Data adds megabytes.
6. **Zero Padding**
   Adding placeholder data to inputs. Padding increases memory megabytes.
7. **Zoomed Feature Maps**
   Scaled representations in vision models. Stored in megabytes.
8. **Zonal Cache**
   Cache divided by region. Cache size is measured in megabytes.
9. **Zero-Day Model Update Size**
   The storage required for emergency updates. Size is measured in megabytes.
10. **Zipped Model Archive**
    Compressed AI model files. Archives reduce megabytes required.

Teacher Implementation Guide

Level 1: Understanding Artificial Narrow Intelligence (ANI)

The Foundation of Modern Artificial Intelligence

Purpose of This Guide

This Teacher Implementation Guide is designed to help educators successfully introduce students to **Artificial Narrow Intelligence (ANI)**—the type of artificial intelligence that powers most of the technologies we interact with today.

The guide provides teachers with:

- Learning goals for each section of the book
- Suggested teaching strategies
- Classroom discussion ideas
- Activities and project suggestions
- Cross-curricular connections
- Assessment guidance

This resource allows the book to function not only as reading material, but as a **complete instructional framework for introducing AI literacy in schools**.

Recommended Grade Levels

This book can be implemented in multiple educational settings:

Middle School (Grades 6–8)
Introduction to AI concepts and digital literacy.

High School (Grades 9–12)
Technology, computer science, and future career exploration.

Early College / Introductory University Courses
Foundations of artificial intelligence and technology studies.

Suggested Course Length

Teachers may use the book in several formats:

4-Week Unit
Introduction to Artificial Intelligence

8-Week Module
AI Literacy and Emerging Technology

16-Week Semester Course
Foundations of Artificial Intelligence

Each chapter can serve as **one lesson or one week of instruction** depending on the depth of discussion and activities.

Learning Goals of the Book

By the end of the course, students should be able to:

Understand what **Artificial Narrow Intelligence (ANI)** is.

Identify how AI systems operate using **data, algorithms, and pattern recognition**.

Recognize how ANI is used in industries such as healthcare, transportation, education, and finance.

Understand the **differences between human intelligence and machine intelligence**.

Discuss ethical challenges such as **bias, privacy, and responsible AI use**.

Explore the future of AI and how students may participate in shaping it.

Teaching Approach

Teachers are encouraged to present this material using an **interactive learning model**.

Recommended instructional methods include:

- Classroom discussion
- Group problem-solving activities
- Technology demonstrations
- Research assignments
- Reflection writing
- Case studies of real-world AI systems

The goal is to help students see that **AI is not abstract science — it is part of everyday life.**

PART I – FOUNDATIONS OF ANI

Chapters 1–4

Teaching Objective

Introduce students to the basic concept of Artificial Narrow Intelligence and how it differs from human thinking.

Chapter 1

Introduction – The World of Artificial Narrow Intelligence

Teacher Focus

Help students recognize how often AI appears in everyday technology.

Examples students may already use:

- YouTube recommendations
- Spotify playlists
- Google search
- Voice assistants
- Smartphone facial recognition

Suggested Activity

Ask students to list **five AI systems they interacted with in the past 24 hours.**

Chapter 2

What Is ANI?

Teacher Focus

Explain the difference between three major types of AI:

• Artificial Narrow Intelligence (ANI)
• Artificial General Intelligence (AGI)
• Artificial Superintelligence (ASI)

Use simple analogies such as:

ANI = a specialist
AGI = a general thinker
ASI = intelligence beyond human capability

Chapter 3

The Mind of a Machine

Teacher Focus

Introduce the concept of:

• algorithms
• data
• pattern recognition

Teachers may compare AI learning to how students learn patterns in math or language.

Chapter 4

How ANI Differs from Human Intelligence

Discussion Topics

What humans can do that machines cannot:

• emotions
• creativity
• empathy
• moral reasoning

Students should understand that **ANI is powerful but limited**.

PART II – ANI IN ACTION

Chapters 5–10

Teaching Objective

Show students how AI is already used across major industries.

Teachers should emphasize **real-world examples**.

Chapter 5

ANI in Education

Possible classroom discussion:

- AI tutoring apps
- adaptive learning platforms
- automated grading tools

Ask students:

"Would AI teachers help or harm education?"

Chapter 6

ANI in Healthcare

Discuss examples such as:

- AI reading X-rays
- cancer detection
- health chatbots

Activity

Students research one medical AI innovation.

Chapter 7

ANI in Transportation

Examples:

• self-driving cars
• traffic optimization
• navigation systems

Discuss how AI reduces accidents and improves logistics.

Chapter 8

ANI in Communication

Examples:

• speech recognition
• translation tools
• voice assistants

Students may test translation tools and compare results.

Chapter 9

ANI in Business and Finance

Examples:

• fraud detection
• stock analysis
• recommendation engines

Teachers can explain how companies use AI to improve efficiency.

Chapter 10

ANI in Entertainment and Media

Examples:

• movie recommendations
• video game AI
• social media algorithms

Students can discuss how algorithms influence what content people see.

PART III – DEEPER UNDERSTANDING

Chapters 11–16

Teaching Objective

Help students think critically about AI's power, limits, and future.

Chapter 11

The Data Behind ANI

Explain:

• datasets
• training data
• testing data

Students should understand that **AI is only as good as the data it learns from**.

Chapter 12

Ethics and Responsibility in ANI

Discussion topics:

• bias in algorithms
• privacy concerns
• responsible AI development

Students can debate real-world AI ethical dilemmas.

Chapter 13

Humans and Machines Working Together

Explain that AI does not replace humans but **augments human capabilities**.

Examples:

• doctors using AI tools
• designers using generative AI
• engineers using machine learning systems.

Chapter 14

Challenges and Limits of ANI

Key concepts:

- ANI cannot think independently
- AI lacks true understanding
- AI cannot form consciousness

Students should understand the difference between **simulation and intelligence**.

Chapter 15

Preparing for the Next Level: From ANI to AGI

Introduce the concept of **Artificial General Intelligence**.

Encourage students to ask:

Will machines ever think like humans?

Chapter 16

The Future of Intelligent Learning

Encourage students to imagine:

- new careers
- new industries
- responsible AI innovation

Teachers may assign a final reflection:

"How will AI shape my future career?"

Suggested Classroom Projects

Teachers may assign projects such as:

AI Observation Journal

Students track AI systems they encounter for one week.

AI Career Research

Students research careers such as:

- AI engineer
- data scientist
- robotics specialist
- AI ethicist

AI Ethics Debate

Students debate questions such as:

Should AI be allowed to make medical decisions?

Assessment Options

Teachers may evaluate student learning through:

- chapter quizzes
- short essays
- presentations
- group projects
- reflective writing

Chapter 17: The Global Impact of ANI

Chapter Overview

Students examine how ANI affects industries, economies, governments, healthcare, education, and daily life around the world.

Key Learning Objectives

Students will:

Identify global applications of ANI.

Understand how AI influences different industries.

Recognize both opportunities and challenges created by AI.

Analyze the worldwide impact of automation.

Discussion Questions

How is ANI changing healthcare?

How is AI transforming education?

What industries are most affected by ANI?

What are the benefits and risks of global AI adoption?

Classroom Activity

Assign groups to research one industry and present how ANI is transforming that sector.

Chapter 18: The Future of Learning in the Age of ANI

Chapter Overview

This chapter explores how AI is changing education through personalized learning, intelligent tutoring systems, adaptive assessments, and new educational technologies.

Key Learning Objectives

Students will:

Explain how AI supports personalized learning.

Identify educational tools powered by ANI.

Discuss the role of teachers in an AI-enhanced classroom.

Understand responsible AI use in education.

Discussion Questions

How can AI help students learn?

Can AI replace teachers? Why or why not?

What are the benefits of personalized learning?

How should students use AI responsibly?

Classroom Activity

Students evaluate an AI-powered educational tool and discuss its strengths and limitations.

Chapter 19: The Human Values Behind ANI

Chapter Overview

Students explore the ethical principles and human values that guide AI development, including fairness, transparency, accountability, privacy, and safety.

Key Learning Objectives

Students will:

Define AI ethics.

Explain why human values matter in AI systems.

Identify examples of bias in AI.

Understand the importance of responsible AI development.

Discussion Questions

Why must AI reflect human values?

What happens when AI systems are biased?

How can developers build fair AI systems?

Who should be responsible for AI decisions?

Classroom Activity

Analyze a hypothetical AI scenario and discuss ethical concerns and possible solutions.

Chapter 20: The Legacy of ANI — Humanity's First Step Toward Conscious Technology

Chapter Overview

The concluding chapter reflects on ANI's historical significance as humanity's first successful generation of intelligent machines and its role in shaping the future of technology and society.

Key Learning Objectives

Students will:

Summarize the major concepts learned throughout the book.

Explain ANI's role in technological history.

Reflect on how AI may shape future generations.

Understand the relationship between human intelligence and machine intelligence.

Discussion Questions

What is ANI's greatest contribution to society?

How has AI changed the world so far?

What lessons should future generations remember about ANI?

What role should humans play in guiding future AI?

Classroom Activity

Students create a "Letter to the Future" describing how they hope AI will be used responsibly in the years ahead.

Final Message for Teachers

Artificial intelligence will shape the future of work, communication, healthcare, and education. By introducing students to Artificial Narrow Intelligence today, educators help prepare the next generation to **understand, guide, and responsibly develop the technologies of tomorrow**.

This book is designed to make AI understandable, accessible, and inspiring for every learner.

www.ingramcontent.com/pod-product-compliance
Lightning Source LLC
Chambersburg PA
CBHW041753220926
51847CB00014B/190
* 9 7 8 1 9 7 2 9 2 5 0 4 1 *